'JESUS IS LORD'

GWENDOLYN SMITH

This book is an accompaniment to the
'Jesus is Lord' Conference ©. The power
of the cross has procured our healing over
the works of the 7-fold strength of evil.

Jesus Is Lord
Copyright © 2016 by Gwendolyn Smith
www.missionacrossborders.co.uk
978-0-9562186-3-6

Published by *Sheba Publications*, July 2016

There can be no great move of God without someone being commissioned to pay the price. His way is marked with suffering and leads to divine purpose.

ACKNOWLEDGEMENT:

I express with sincere thanks to Jesus my Lord that He is the Truth and the Living One. It is God who has given unto me this ministry of healing and reconciliation.

Unique to the call is the way in which the number 7 has featured throughout the preparation for this ministry. It is undoubtedly a mystery, but God continues to bear out figuratively His *perfect finished plan* for the salvation of mankind symbolised by a mark of the number 7 that denotes completion.

I therefore, humbly acknowledge that this is an end-time ministry leading up to the rapture of the saints.

God alone is able to bring back from the brink the broken pieces of our lives and put the entities of human life back together again. Restored to wholeness and recovered to the eternal state that God had in mind from the beginning of time.

God can do all things and no purposes of His can be thwarted by evil. (Job 42:1). Therefore, I decree healing of all entities of life from here on in the name of Jesus who is Lord over all realms and kingdoms.

Author's Comment

God revealed to me that the book entitled *15 Minute Prayer Strategy for Families* was the focus for the 7-year testing.

I remember clearly, the day He prompted me to write that first book in 2008. I did not start out with any idea of what to write, but I ended up with a book stating unequivocally the power of God to heal all areas of life. My life immediately came under an evil attack, and I was fighting for everything that constituted the entirety of my life. Yet, God just kept telling me to keep going and to trust Him.

Once again, I am under an incredibly compelling urge to write. God gave me 7 books and this book is entitled "Jesus is Lord."

Faith is inextricably linked to divine healing. That first book stated categorically that Jesus is Healer. The fact that I stood on the integrity of the Word and endured suffering at the hands of my enemies is the divine faith that prompts God to act. Without faith, it is impossible to please God. God required me to exercise the level of faith that would cause Him to move on my behalf as He did to all those who came to Him for deliverance and healing.

I have no doubt that there is now a shift in the order of my life. I had to trust God to help me survive the challenges of the testing. It was a season that was incredibly personal, deeply wounding and the challenges immensely complex. In fact, since 2015 when the season of breakthrough commenced, I have come to realise that the journey to bringing order back to one's life is as hugely challenging as the season of loss.

The wells of experience were immensely deep, and I needed divine help to extricate my life from the depths of such despair. The Psalmist David said of those who had risen up against him that they were mightier than he. He stated that his enemies had banded against him as a "bond of wickedness." Only God can disperse the syndicates of evil assigned against your life.

My faith has now soared through testing, and I continue to express God's unquestionable ability to heal all entities of human life based on His Word. Today, the spiritual yoke of testing has expanded and given way as God revealed to me that it was a *7-year season of testing and preparation.* I am now in the 8th year of the spiritual journey. I survived! Thank God!

It is now a season of "New Beginnings"!

PREFACE:

This book is based on what God has given to me to prepare me for His service. It is primarily for those who will come to salvation in this end season of grace. Particularly those of other faiths who are seeking to understand about Jesus as Lord, and His work of deliverance for the healing of mankind.

AUTHOR'S NOTE:

The journey to becoming fully equipped for the next level of fight has been spiritually demanding, emotionally charged, and physically horrendous. It has taken every ounce of me. The person, Gwendolyn, whom family and friends knew, died in the suffering. A new and transformed life has emerged from the experiences of a life once lived. I was reduced to absolute nothingness in order for God to increase in me.

I will not shift my confidence in God. *"Jesus is Lord"* over every kingdom, realm, and nation. He alone has the power to bring divine order to all entities of human life. His will be done now on earth as it is in heaven.

TABLE OF CONTENTS

INTRODUCTION

I remember very early on in the inception of this ministry that someone placed a Derek Prince book in my hand, '*He Came To Set The Captives Free*'. From reading the first couple of chapters, I began to get a sense of where God was directing me and why I was under such extreme spiritual challenges. God had called me to the ministry of healing and restoration of His promises. Anyone who will take up the mantle and follow the example of the Lord, giving priority to the deliverance of the people from the snares of the evil fowler will be subject to strong hostility from the enemy.

What else could stir the spirits of evil to oppose the work of God? It can only be because the adversary wants people to remain in their spiritual bondage. The liberating power of God will set the captives free. That is what Jesus was about in His ministry of reconciliation. His mandate is to restore all things back to the divine order of His grace. It must be stated unequivocally that we are in the time of accelerated grace because mankind must be delivered from the power of sin. The end-time outpouring of salvation and healing is upon us and the time is short. It will be awesome like no other period in the history of mankind as we approach the season of the coming of our Lord.

The people coming under easy surrender to sin are not the intended targets. We come under attack for the kingdom's sake. The people are just the "pawns" used by the enemy to accomplish his plans. Ultimately, the kingdom of God is a threat to the adversary and because the kingdom of God is within man, we are relentlessly pursued to fail in our Christian walk.

Jesus is the giver of life, born to rule with the sceptre of righteousness and truth. The plan of the evil one is to forbid the advancement of His kingdom in the hearts of men. *"For to us a child is born, to us a son is given; and the government shall be upon his shoulder, and his name shall be called Wonderful*

Counselor, Mighty God, Everlasting Father, Prince of Peace, of the increase of his government and of peace there will be no end" *(Isaiah 9:6,7 ESV).* When we understand the strategies of Satan and remain stoic in the Word, we counter his moves against the ultimate work of the Lord here on earth. To exercise the authority assigned to us by God for the mandated territories of souls, it will undoubtedly elicit a backlash from the foe.

Jesus came to set men free from every form of spiritual captivity. His Word was sent to rescue people from the pits of destruction they fall into. It is a spiritual fight as men are under the burden of the law until they come to the knowledge of the truth concerning salvation. The work of Satan is to keep the people entrenched in spiritual bondage. It is a tight grip of fear and ignorance described as a gross spiritual darkness enveloping the world.

To know *Jesus as Lord* is to be triumphant over the works of evil.

PART ONE
THE MINISTRY OF JESUS

"He sent His Word to heal us and to rescue us from every pit"

(Psalms 107:20, ESV)

1.1 The Lion of Judah

Jesus came from the lineage of Judah. The tribe of Judah was blessed to rule as kings. They were aggressive and persistent in enemy combat. After the death of Joshua, God chose Judah to become the fighting force to drive out the inhabitants of the land he had commissioned for Israel. *(1) "After the death of Joshua, the people of Israel inquired of the LORD, 'Who shall go up first for us against the Canaanites, to fight against them?' (2)The LORD said, 'Judah shall go up; behold, I have given the land into his hand'" (Judges 1:1-2, ESV).* Judah, strong and militant prevailed against their enemies conquering the Canaanites in the southern tip of the land to secure it.

Jacob's blessing to Judah illustrates the warrior spirit of Judah. He uses the analogy of the lion, the most majestic and predatory of beasts to describe their tribal characteristics. *"Judah you are ye whom your brothers shall praise; your hand shall be on the neck of your enemies; your father's children shall bow down before you. Judah is a lion's whelp; from the prey, my son, you have gone up. He bows down, he lies down as a lion; and as a lion, who shall rouse him? The sceptre shall not depart from Judah, nor a lawgiver from between his feet, until Shiloh comes, and to Him shall be the obedience of the people " (Genesis 49:8-10).* As a clan, they would fight relentlessly for what was rightfully theirs. They were also entrusted with writing and keeping the oracles of God. They would fight tenaciously to keep the law and its promises until Jesus whose right it is comes as recorded in the prophecies to be fulfilled. The word *Shiloh* is an untranslated Hebrew expression meaning "the one to whom it belongs. " The prophecies were guarded and preserved, shrouded in mystery until Jesus came to fulfill them and usher in a new and living way. In John 5:22, we see that everything belongs to Jesus because the Father has given Him authority as ruler over all things. Only *Yeshua Ha- Mashiach* was found worthy in the heavens to open the seven seals. *"And one of the elders saith unto me, Weep not: the lion of the tribe of Judah, the root of David, hath prevailed to open the book, and to loose the seven seals thereof." (Revelation 5:5) KJV.*

1.2   The Prevailer

Yeshua the Messiah, Jesus our Lord prevailed against the forces of darkness for our redemption. Like Judah, He is referred to as the Lion of Judah who conquers in the spirit realm to break every chain of bondage. His eminence over their evil works brought our deliverance as He triumphantly secured our victory at the cross. Jesus often sought out privacy in the Garden of Gethsemane. It would have been a preferred location for Him. A quiet area situated alongside the Brook Kidron and Mount Olives in the proximity of Jerusalem. It was here that He would agonise through the long night before He willingly offered Himself as the sacrificial Lamb of God for the sins of the people.

The word *Gethsemane* is a Hebrew word according to *Strongs 1068* and when broken into two it provides a clearer meaning. *Gat* is to "press*" and *semane* means "oil." It was on that lonely hillside of Mount Olives in the favoured garden that Jesus spent His last night before the crucifixion travailing and pressing through in the Spirit. One can draw parallels with the weight of His suffering and the heavy stone slabs in the olive press that crushed the tender fruits. It was that spiritual fight to prevail over the works of darkness that has released us from the oppressive force of evil assigned against our world.

1.3   An Eternal Priesthood

Jesus, a Prophet sent from God occupied a dual office being also an eternal Priest and the Messiah, our soon coming King. He is called our Great High Priest who opened up the way of salvation to mankind. Jesus was not from the ancestry of the Aaronic priesthood who were called to service in the temple. Aaron was a Levite whose family was chosen by God to dedicate themselves purely to matters pertaining to the Priesthood. *"And the Lord spoke to Aaron saying, drink no wine or strong drink, you or your sons with you, when you go into the tent of meeting, lest you die. It shall be a statute forever throughout your generations. You are to distinguish between the holy and the common, and between the unclean and the clean, and you are to teach the people of Israel all the statutes that the LORD has spoken to them by Moses."(Leviticus 10:8-11, ESV).* Jesus, a Nazarene came from the tribe of Judah.

Jesus was born to rule and when He was brought into the house of the Lord to be blessed, the priest read from the Book of the Law what was written by Moses, *"As it is written in the Law of the Lord, 'Every male who first opens the womb shall be called holy to the Lord'" (Luke 2:23, ESV).* Being the only begotten Son of God, the only one of God to be born in the natural realm, He opened up the eternal womb of salvation and healing for the nations.

The ministry of Jesus is as the Chief High Priest according to (Hebrews 5:1-5) *"For every high priest chosen from among men is appointed to act on behalf of men in relation to God, to offer gifts and sacrifices for sins. He can deal gently with the ignorant and wayward since he himself is beset with weakness. Because of this, he is obligated to offer sacrifice for his own sins just as he does for those of the people. And no one takes this honor for himself, but only when called by God, just as Aaron was. So also Christ did not exalt himself to be made a high priest, but was appointed by him who said to him, 'Thou art my Son, today have I begotten thee.'"* The apostle Paul eminently outlined his argument that Jesus met the *7-fold* qualifications for the priesthood. He affirms that under the old order the priest must:-

- be chosen from amongst the people
- be selected for the benefit and welfare of the people
- be chosen by God for His service
- offer sacrifices for the sins of the people
- be patient with the errant ways of the people

4

- recognise his own weaknesses and failings
- also offer sacrifice for himself

Paul made the case for Jesus meeting the criteria above and also superceding the requirements. Firstly, Jesus came in the flesh to save mankind, to experience life and its challenges as we do. His ministry is all the more credible because He suffered as do humankind against the evil one. The Bible said that He was tempted as we were yet without sin. He was wounded for our transgressions. By the stripes He suffered, we are delivered from sinful bondages, healed in our spirit and the fragmented soul is made whole. He cared enough for mankind to willingly offer Himself on the cross.

He was sent from God and sought only to do service unto God. Through His death, the strength of sin that was against us has been abolished. It was the one and only sacrifice needed for mankind's sin. Because He was in the flesh, He would spend long spiritually demanding times in the presence of God. *"In the days of his flesh, Jesus offered up prayers and supplications, with loud cries and tears, to him who was able to save him from death, and he was heard because of his reverence." (Hebrew 5:7, ESV).* He is the eternal mediator between God and man reconciling us back to His Father's love. He pleads daily on our behalf ever loving and faithful to forgive us when we fall short of His glory.

It is without a doubt that Jesus' life attests to Him being the Chief of the High Priesthood. *"Seeing then that we have a great high priest, that is passed into the heavens, Jesus the Son of God, let us hold fast our profession. For we have not a high priest who cannot be touched with the feelings of our infirmities; but was in all points tested like as we are, yet without sin. Let us therefore come boldly unto the throne of grace, that we may obtain mercy, and find grace to help in time of need. (Hebrews 4:14-16).* As our heavenly Priest, His earthly service was undertaken, devoid of the religious burdens associated with rituals, sacrifices, and ceremonies. His love for the people went beyond the form and the norm. He was a priest not from the earthly Aaronic order but after the eternal order of Melchizedek. *"You are my Son, today I have begotten you; as he says also in another place, "You are a priest forever, after the order of Melchizedek."* (Hebrews 5:6). Melchizedek was mentioned briefly in the Scriptures as having no beginning or end of days. It is quite evident that Melchizedek and Jesus are one of the same according to contemporary writers.

1.4   The Deliverer of the People

The word *sozo* in Greek terminology *(Strong's 4982)* means 'to deliver and make whole'. It is the root word of *soter (Strong's 4990)* meaning 'Saviour'. Jesus is the Saviour who is the deliverer and healer of the people. Christ became a curse by hanging on a tree so that the works of evil could be laid bare at the cross. *"Christ hath redeemed us from the curse of the law, being made a curse for us: for it is written, Cursed is every one that hangeth on a tree" (Galatians 3:13, KJV).*

The human race has been subjected to the bondage of the curse from the time of creation. God instituted in the law given to His people, the ceremonial order for the disposal of a person hung on a tree in order that the land is not defiled by the curse that the deceased person is under. *"You are not to leave his corpse on the tree overnight but are to bury him that day, for anyone hung on a tree is under God's curse. You must not defile the land the LORD your God is giving you as an inheritance" (Deuteronomy 21:23, Holmans).*

The suffering of Jesus characterises the role of a prophet chosen by God. In His humiliated state, they crucified Him and placed Him in a grave, but as recorded in the Scriptures, He rose again. *"That he was buried, that he was raised on the third day in accordance with the Scriptures" (1 Corinthians 15:4, ESV).*

Jesus became the burden bearer for sin. He knew rejection at the cross when His father momentarily moved away from Him before He gave up His spirit and died. It must have been the loneliest journey to the cross and the most painful separation imaginable. It was only that powerful and complete work of divine grace that could have broken the fetters that bound us to the curse of sin.

The Lord has procured our spiritual healing at Calvary. It was through His benevolent act of grace that we are saved. His eternal purpose is to bring healing and deliverance to a fallen world. He has redeemed our souls from all spiritual captivities designed against us. Every form of spiritual bondage has been nailed to the cross, and we are eternally liberated from the clutches of the evil one.

The power of the evil spiritual realm has been broken by the greater formidable power of God. The indelible marks of sin's curse were etched deeply in our being. The blood of the eternal "Lamb" has erased every stain. The heavy chains that held men eternally captive have been broken and destroyed. It took Jesus, the Son of God who is the Saviour of the world, to become the perfect sacrifice for sin. He is the sacrificial Lamb chosen of God. He came into this world once to die for mankind. His death has served for all time as the potently effective sacrifice that was offered for us. It was the ultimate price that could be paid for our sins. He suffered the public shame afforded convicts, yet, He opened not His mouth to retaliate. He was mistreated and reduced to nothingness by His enemies. He was finally nailed to a cross alongside common criminals. In the earth realm, that was the harrowing scene depicted at the cross.

1.5   Triumphant Lord

However, in the heavens, it was a cause for celebration as God the Father revealed to man the eternal glory of His Son, our risen Lord Jesus. In the offering of Himself for the sins of the world, He completed the great eternal plan of salvation. It is the only message of eternal hope for a lost world.

In His glorious exalted position as Lord, He conquered over hell, death, and the grave. He released the captives from the curse of sin and vanquished His foe. The Scriptures record that He took the keys of death and hell and as conqueror over these entities of human bondage, He prevailed against Satan. He nailed to the cross all that would chain us to the destroying force of sin and freed men from every abyss of destruction.

As a Prophet sent by God, Jesus is the divine deity who entered the earth realm as the son born to a virgin girl of Jewish descent. Mary, who came from the lineage of Judah was chosen above all women to be the mother of our Lord. In the form of humankind, Jesus was destined with a divine mandate to bring the world to salvation. He would tabernacle in the hearts of men and thereby set up the reign of His spiritual kingdom in our being. He now reigns in those who have given their hearts as a place of His worship. The heart becomes the living tabernacle of His Holy Presence.

What rejoicing, as the work of grace was accomplished and eternally sealed in the heavens! The eternal gates of praise were lifted up for the King of Glory to enter in. Jesus returned triumphantly to His Father in heaven. He is now seated at the right hand of God. At the time of His Second Advent to earth as the Messiah, reigning King of kings, He will destroy His enemies. His justice will then be poured out upon the nations and those who rejected the eternal hope we have in Him.

1.6   A Prophet Sent by God

In The New Testament, the people affirmed Jesus as a Prophet living amongst them. *"And the crowds said, 'This is the prophet Jesus, from Nazareth of Galilee,'".(Matthew 21:11, ESV).* The witness of Jesus as Healer, Deliverer and Saviour is evident through His works amongst the people.

We who have come to salvation have a sure foundation in Jesus Christ. Jesus is the chief capstone that underpins the spiritual building of our faith. His eternal support of the kingdom cannot be destroyed or eroded by sin. It is durably strong against all demonic assaults. We are co-workers in God's service. We are God's field. God's building. The Patron of our faith is qualified and substantiated by the prophetic words written of Him in scripture. We are bastions of the faith knowing that our foundation in Jesus is built on the infallible proof of those credible scriptures. *" Having being built on the foundation of the apostles and the prophets, the Messiah Jesus himself being the cornerstone" (Ephesians 2:20, ISV).*

1.7   The Call of a Prophet

The office of the prophet is primarily one of healing. It is not to be confused with the gift of prophecy. Many people operate in the gift of prophecy. The gift is manifested through dreams, visions, and revelations. Others may have the gift to see things concerning the state of people's lives and be able to give them a word to help them. However, these spiritual abilities are all features of the prophetic.

The role of the prophet chosen by God differs to a prophetic gift. The prophet is a vessel chosen by God. The person entrusted with the office will have no doubt concerning the call. A prophet serves for a particular season and time, usually in a time of great national crisis. God will ensure the prophet is equipped for his/her remit. One will be given a level of operation or assignment essential to the call. It is God's love for mankind that moves Him to commission a chosen vessel for a strategic call.

The prophet is authorised by God to be His instrument and mouthpiece in the earth. God will tell his prophet or speak through His chosen vessel what to say. *"I will raise them up a Prophet from among their brethren, like unto thee, and will put my words in his mouth; and he shall speak unto them all that I shall command him " (Deuteronomy 18:18, KJV).* He will also tell you to what jurisdiction and purpose He has called you to serve. The prophetic call is usually in a strategic role over regions, nations or within a global context of operation. *"See, I have set you this day over nations and over kingdoms, to pluck up and to break down, to destroy and to overthrow, to build and to plant." (Jeremiah 1:10, ESV).*

Jesus commissioned the twelve disciples to move out of their comfort zones, healing the sick and spreading the Good News. He cautioned them to take no script or provision because God is their provider. In Matthew 10:16 he warns them to be shrewd but harmless as doves because they will be operating among their enemies. There would be no need to worry when they are betrayed and brought before the council of leaders. He reminds them that the Holy Spirit will speak for them in that hour of testing. The prophet will suffer as Jesus suffered.

Before a prophet is called into service they undergo rigorous training by God. The time of preparation is usually long and lonely. Essential to the call is the need to spend much time praying and seeking instructions from the Lord. God releases the person called to the prophetic office only when they have qualified through testing and preparation. He remains with the prophet throughout their earthly assignment giving instructions and directing their way. *"No man shall be able to stand before you all the days of your life. Just as I was with Moses, so I will be with you. I will not leave you or forsake you." (Joshua 1:5 ESV.)* It is not the desire of God that they fail in their assignment because they are commissioned and sent out unprepared. No! God loves His servant and an incredibly special bond is developed over the course of the assignment. You will have no doubt when God has chosen you.

A prophet is often misunderstood by the mass and their mission usually requires them to be set apart for the service of God. Jesus said of the prophet that he would have no honour amongst his own people. He drew reference to Himself as He experienced rejection by the Jews. The experiences of Jesus epitomise the office of a prophet because the same devil is behind the rejection of those chosen. The life of the one chosen is marred with pain and suffering, public humiliation and despair. By the time God is ready to bring you out, you are "broken in" as a horse subdued for service.

Prophets undertake missions that require great test of faith depending solely on the Eternal One who chose them for His service. Trusting in God under spiritual challenges takes great faith supported by the Spirit of God. The Scriptures say that without faith it is impossible to please God. It is without a doubt that the prophet has to know the voice of God distinct to any other voice. It is that dependency and trusting in God in a time of crisis that weighs heavily on the servant of God to make decisive and timely responses according to God's leading. If a prophet is not hearing from God then it is without doubt that another spirit is at work. Indeed, Jesus warned His disciples of the false prophets who would come looking like sheep but their inward traits are those of a wolf seeking to devour unwary lambs.

1.8   Season of False Prophets

There is no mention of a named prophet since the time of Christ, however, the new and living way has made it possible for all to operate to a lesser or greater degree in the prophetic stream. There are prophets today who are called by God to strategic ministries whereby He directs the assignment. The bible makes much mention of the false prophets that will arise in the last days, endowed with a spirit of seduction. They will seek to assert their own will to deceive the people of God with their trickery and sleek charisma.

The spirit of error and falsehood is undoubtedly prevalent in this closing age of grace. The spirit of heresy and idolatry are termed as iniquities simply because they are ingrained and rooted through years of rebellion. When God shows us our weaknesses and sins, we must confess them and repent. If we continue to disobey the bidding of the Spirit, we will fall into another category of sinfulness. It is the doctrinal errors that one holds that will become embedded with time. The tenacious grip of heresy is a strong demon and once it has taken hold, it seeks to destroy the victim under the bondage of pride. The spirit of error is particularly active in seeking to destroy the ministers of God. The position of authority they hold is conducive to propagating the seeds of doctrinal error across a great sway of the body of Christ, misleading many.

Jesus said that many false prophets would come in His name. *"For false christs and false prophets will arise and perform great signs and wonders, so as to lead astray, if possible, even the elect" (Matthew 24:24, ESV).* Spirits of error and falsehood are unteachable spirits with maverick tendencies. Because they are false prophets, they will operate as predatory lone wolves. Prophets are loners but without the leading of God, they are in effect diviners and not prophets. *(29) "I know that after my departure fierce wolves will come in among you, not sparing the flock; (30) and from among your own selves will arise men speaking twisted things, to draw away the disciples after them"* (Acts 20:29-30, ESV). The line between the prophet and the diviner is very thin. It is only the Spirit of God with the perfect 7-fold vision of God who is able to keep His servant pure and uncontaminated from the pollution of these end-time spirits.

For by their characteristics, we shall know their breeding. One of their traits is that they are not teachable, speaking from the abundance of their heart. By their fruits, we shall know them. *(18) "Children, it is the last hour, and as you have heard that antichrist is coming, so now many antichrists have come. Therefore we know that it is the last hour. (19) They went out from us, but they were not of us; for if they had been of us, they would have continued with us. But they went out, that it might become plain that they all are not of us"* (1 John 2:18-19, ESV).

The Word clearly states what God detests concerning the false prophet. *"Therefore, behold I am against the prophets, declares the Lord..."* (Jeremiah 23:30, ESV).

These are the *7-fold* sins of the prophets of Samaria and Jerusalem.

1.   They steal God's words everyone from his neighbour.

2.   They use their tongues and say, *"God said."*

3.   They prophesy lying dreams.

4.   They tell their lying dreams and cause the people to err.

5.   They speak lies through boasting.

6.   They have not been sent out by God.

7.   They do not know the burden of Jehovah God.

Jesus Himself was a prophet and throughout His earthly ministry, He showed by example how important it was to be connected to the source for the work of God. We are employed in the service of God. It is God who has the eternal vision and at His bidding, we operate within our prophetic gifts. *"For I have come down from heaven, not to do my own will but the will of him who sent me" (John 6:38, ESV).*

Jesus knew the burden of the Father, and it often caused Him to separate Himself from the disciples and the multitudes to be alone with God. In dealing with the religious cohorts of leaders, He would become frustrated and angry at their lack of compassion towards the needy folks. I believe it is the single most important message Jesus has shown through the gospels that the people were as lost sheep without a shepherd. It caused Him much sadness of heart.

1.9 Intimacy in Prayer

The office of the prophet requires long periods spent in the presence of the Lord. As a prophet, we see that Jesus was dishonoured, publicly humiliated, and suffered physical abuse by the people He came to deliver. He was purposed to effectuate the work of grace thereby building His kingdom in the hearts of the people. His role required Him to be alone with His Father for extenuating periods of time. Being the burden bearer of mankind, the intensity of the weight placed upon Him drove Him into solitary places where with strong crying, He prevailed against the powers of darkness. It is an incredibly lonely call as God directs His prophet into His presence to hear from Him and feel the burden He feels for the people.

The Scriptures illustrate clearly how Jesus would remove Himself from the throng of needy people and from His disciples to spend isolated times in long prayers and intimacy with God. *"And it came to pass in those days, that he went out into a mountain to pray and continued all night in prayer to God" (Luke 6:12, KJV).* On this occasion, He came back from His night of vigil knowing those He would choose as the twelve apostles to carry on His kingdom work when He left them to go back to His Father. The time spent with God is intended to know the mind of God concerning His will being done in the earth. Jesus is depicted as a poignantly pitiful figure of a man laden with the spiritual burden of mankind. Isaiah 53 reveals the suffering servant who would agonise in prayer and prevail over the realm of evil to procure our redemption.

It is a life characterised by the demonstration of God's power working through the individual. Being set apart for the service often makes them appear unusually different. Therefore, the prophet is inclined to display cautiously restrained and watchful tendencies as people try to make sense of them. An impromptu move or mistake in obedience to God could have far-reaching consequences. Yet our God is a merciful God knowing the weaknesses of His servants. It is imperative that the individual chosen remains steadfast at the feet of Jesus.

Jesus said of Himself that, *"My food is to do the will of him who sent me and to accomplish his work" (John 4:34, ESV).* He made God's business His priority. He only spoke and acted on what God determined. A prophet is essentially an ambassador, working under the auspices of God's leading with the divine covering of God.

1.10   Blighted by Sin

Sin is like a tap-root spreading across and through the soil. Sin has pervaded all entities of human life bringing misery and discomfort. Sin is like a spiritually hardy fibrous root reaching deep into the soul of man. It produces the fruits of unrighteousness. The curse of sin is endemic to all mankind and has been passed through a spiritually legal covenant. Adam and Eve, our fore-parents listened to the Devil guised as a serpent and they sinned against God. Using his charm, Satan disarmed them and convinced them that if they ate of the tree they would not die. Indeed, they did not die physically but a *spiritual death* was passed to mankind. God cursed mankind by His decree, *"I will put enmity between you and the woman and between your offspring and her offspring; he shall bruise your head and you shall bruise his heel (Genesis 3:15).*

To counter the curse, Jesus who is known figuratively as the "Lamb of God" became the sacrificial beast of burden for the sins of the world. He pulled the heavy weight of the cross, symbolic of the weight of our sins up to Golgotha's hill, whilst being mercilessly trashed by the people. Through His selfless act of dying for mankind, we can spiritually live again. *"God sent his own son in the likeness of sinful man to be a sin offering" (Romans 8:3). "I am the resurrection and the life though he were dead yet shall he live" (John 11:25-26).*

1.11   Breaking The Curse

There is no waste in the cycle of nature. Continuity is hardwired into creation for the survival of the species. Out of one single seed that dies, a proliferation of seeds occurs producing many new shoots. Jesus' death produced many after His kind. God's Word in creation ensured that Jesus would bring continuity of spiritual life in mankind. Hence, Jesus, through His death ensured the permanence and progression of His kingdom of righteousness that knows no end.

Jesus was the only one found worthy to open the seal of redemption to break the curse of sin and free the oppressed *(Revelation 5:4).* His willing posture of servitude at the cross, culminated in the death of the "perfect lamb" for the sins of the world. On one occasion, when John the Baptist set eyes on Jesus he proclaimed, *"Behold, the Lamb of God, who takes away the sin of the world!" (John 1:29, ESV).* There could be no life except our deliverance from the curse was secured at the cross and Jesus' power stripped away the legal strongholds keeping people bound in their spiritual captivity.

His death and resurrection removed the gross spiritual darkness that encircled our wretched lives. The darkness is an oppressive spiritual gloom penetrating the being. Only God can access the dim regions of the heart where evil lurks. Jesus our Lord has the power to break the fetters to set the people free from their captivity and to heal their wounds. *"O LORD my God, I cried out to you, and you healed me" (Psalm 30:2, ESV).* Jesus is referred to as the "sent one," a Prophet sent from God to heal the people from their sins when they cry unto Him.

Millions of people have come to know the renewing, healing power of the cross being lived out in their lives daily. *"Jesus broke the law of sin that was making us prisoners of sin" (Romans 7:23, NIV).* Jesus has destroyed every power that could possibly hold us in the spiritual strangleholds of life. It is a cause for celebration because we are truly released from a lifetime of sin's bondage through the death of our Lord Jesus.

1.12   Proclaiming Liberty

The Scriptures qualify the mandate given to Jesus that He would break the bars of the spiritual prisons to free the oppressed that are distressed by sin. He came to the earth and the prophecies concerning Him were fulfilled. It was foretold that He would come, *"To open the eyes that are blind, to bring out the prisoners from the dungeon, from the prison those who sit in darkness. I am the LORD; that is my name; my glory I give to no other, nor my praise to carved idols. Behold, the former things have come to pass, and new things I now declare; before they spring forth I tell you of them." (Isaiah 21:7-9, ESV).*

After Jesus was tempted by the Devil in the wilderness on this particular day, we see as was His habit that He went into the temple. The scrolls of the prophet Isaiah were given to Him to read. *(17) "The scroll of the prophet Isaiah was handed to him. Unrolling it, he found the place where it is written: (18) The Spirit of the Lord is on me, because he has anointed me to preach good news to the poor. He has sent me to proclaim freedom for the prisoners and recovery of sight for the blind, to release the oppressed" (Luke 4:17-18, ESV).* The prophecy of Him being the Deliverer was now fulfilled. The promised Holy One was now standing before their very eyes. His time had come to take up His mantle.

The Bible said the anointing was strong upon Him having just ended forty days of fasting. That which was written of Him as the Deliverer of the people was now embodied in the flesh before those present in the temple. He would break every chain of bondage and redeem lost souls from the kingdom of darkness into His kingdom of light. Jesus the Deliverer was ready to commence His earthly ministry of reconciliation and healing.

1.13   The Kingdom of Light

The Scripture clearly outlines that sin is universal. *"See, darkness covers the earth and thick darkness is over the peoples, but the LORD rises upon you and his glory appears over you" (Isaiah 60:2, NIV)*. The glory of Jesus is that light that shines in the regions of darkness. If sin is universal, then the antidote to its poison is salvation, the universal cure. It has been made available to all peoples on the face of the earth who will repent and come to Jesus Christ.

Satan's influence over mankind has propagated seeds of destruction in all aspects of human life but the kingdom of light has brought hope. *"To whom God would make known what is the riches of the glory of this mystery among the Gentiles; which is Christ in you, the hope of glory" (Colossians 1:27, KJV)*. This hope shines in us and is Jesus Christ Himself. Paul the apostle refers to the mystery of the great privilege given to the Gentiles that they can share in the resurrection hope of Jesus living inside of His people. That which was first to the Jews, perversely slighted has been made available to the Gentiles. It is indeed a mystery because it cannot be entertained unless one has the witness through salvation. It is a glorious hope that shines in the dark regions of the foreboding deep of the soul. It radiates the works of God's kingdom of light that is the righteousness of His Word.

1.14   Reconciled to God

The ministry of reconciliation is ultimately the work of salvation and healing. It is Jesus who brought salvation and mankind are the object of His deliverance. He alone has the power to deliver men from sin. He willingly came to set us free from the burdens of our captivity. Salvation is deliverance because we are first saved from the clutches of the enemy and redeemed unto God through Jesus, His beloved Son.

By being reconciled to God, we become servants of the righteousness of God. Jesus instructed His disciples who were recipients of the promise to go and make disciples. He called them from their daily livelihood of mending nets and fishing in the same familiar waters into spiritually deep waters where the catch was greater, more diverse and immensely challenging. We are called to the spiritual pool to fish for the souls of men. It becomes more testing because we must contend with the evil hunter fishing in the same waters seeking to ensnare and destroy the lives of men.

Humanity can come to the knowledge of the divine truth concerning God's existential plan for man. We can come to that place of reconciling our ignorance with our purpose of life. It is ultimately to be made right with God and heal the rift that sin brought about in the lives of men.

Through Jesus Christ, we are forgiven and justified by faith. We are released from all captivities of sin. Jesus was given the power and the authority by God to break the eternal yokes of sin and set the captives free from the snare of the adversary. *"And Jesus came and said to them, 'All authority in heaven and on earth has been given to me.'" (Matthew 28:18,ESV)*. No one can dispute the authenticity of the Son of God. The Scriptures are infallible proof of His divine entity, His earthly lineage, and purpose.

Jesus' mandate is to restore all things back to the Father in the fullness of time. All that was lost through sin can be recovered through the ministry of reconciliation. *"All this is from God, who through Christ reconciled us to himself and gave us the ministry of reconciliation" (2 Corinthians 5:18, ESV).* We, therefore, pray this verse of scripture that God be glorified in the earth. *"Thy will be done on earth as it is in heaven."* It is the will of the Father that mankind once more can have an intimate relationship with Him as He had with Adam and Eve before the fall from grace. For there is no other name given to man for the redemption of sin. Being reconciled to God can only be made possible through His Son Jesus Christ. That great work of grace can now be replicated in the lives of countless others around this globe, as we seek to impart the Word to lost souls still under the yoke of sin.

1.15   Spirit of Delusion

Those who claim to know God outside of His Son are under the spirit of delusion. It is a strong insidious spirit that destroys truth from the mind of the victim. There are strong forces behind the spirit of delusion. These dark forces are at work to prevent people from coming to the knowledge of Jesus as their Lord to bring salvation and divine healing.

The Word of God is accurate and explicit in bearing truth to the line of command concerning Jesus Christ. He said to His accusers *"I am the way and the truth and the life. No one comes to the Father except through me" (John 14:6, NIV).* Indeed, they did not know God the Father. If they did, they would have known that Jesus was the way to eternal life because He said in verse 7, *"If you had known me you would have known the Father also."* That truth still stands sure today in the time of great confusion concerning who Jesus is. You cannot know God unless you first accept Jesus as Lord. Those who want to sidestep Jesus to go to God are undoubtedly under a strong delusion and their efforts to find God are futile. They remain in gross darkness concerning the Heavenly Father because they reject His Son, Jesus.

It is the strategy of the deceiver of the people to bring confusion concerning Jesus and His authority to transform and make whole the lives of people. When Jesus expelled the evil spirits from the mute and blind demon-possessed man, the crowd rightly gave acknowledgement to Jesus as being the Son of David. It was that reference that incurred the fury of the Pharisees to question amongst each other by what authority He healed the man. They conferred that He could only have driven out the demon by the authority of Beelzebub. Jesus quieted their foolish talk by saying, "A house that is divided against itself will come to ruin because the kingdom of demons cannot work against itself." *(24)* *"But when the Pharisees heard it, they said, 'It is only by Beelzebub, the prince of demons, that this man casts out demons.' (25) Knowing their thoughts, he said to them, "Every kingdom divided against itself is laid waste, and no city or house divided against itself will stand" (Matthew 12:24-25, ESV).* Satan's kingdom is a strategic one, and they succeed in their effort because they unite as a whole entity. The only way the church can stand against this principality is to be united as one in Christ Jesus. It is the Spirit of God who will initiate and galvanise the efforts of the church to a place of enviable authority in this world.

PART TWO
JESUS THE DELIVERER

"The Spirit of the Lord is upon me, because he has anointed me to proclaim good news to the poor. He has sent me to proclaim liberty to the captives and recovering of sight to the blind, to set at liberty those who are oppressed,"

(Luke 4:18, ESV)

2.1   The Keeper of the Soul

Jesus the Christ is mankind's deliverer. The meaning of deliverer is derived from the Greek word *soter (Strong's (4990).* It translates "a saviour or preserver." Jesus brought salvation to man and His power is potent to preserve us from the contaminants of sin in the earth. It is the weaknesses of the flesh that the enemy uses to entrap us to sin. The power of the Holy Spirit is sufficient to keep our hearts and minds in the will of God. Jesus said to His disciples that He would be going away from their presence. He would send the "bearer of truth," namely the Comforter. The Holy Spirit would continue the great work of healing and as the revealer of truth, He would teach us how to live holy unto God. *"Training us to renounce ungodliness and worldly passions, and to live self-controlled, upright, and godly lives in the present age" (Titus 2:12, ESV).* Through Jesus, we can be kept from the spiritual deterioration that sin brings. The narrative in scripture of the Messiah, the Anointed One is that He would come and bring healing to the people. His ultimate purpose is to release men from their captivity and in so doing we are spiritually reconciled to the Father.

2.2   Diseased and Ostracised

The original word *lepra* is termed "leprosy" in Greek translation *(Strong's 3014).* The word *lepra* according to Strong's covers a whole range of skin diseases and therefore, not solely referring to leprosy whereby the diseased person is ostracised from the community until such time as they are cured. For example, according to 2 Kings 5, it appears that Naaman, the Syrian leader was able to continue interacting with people and living a relatively normal life. Yet, the Bible refers to him as having leprosy. I guess his variant of leprosy may not have required him to be certified "unclean" warranting him to be banished outside of the city for a period of time. So, it is safe to say that the word "leprosy" in bible times was used as a generic reference to a wide range of skin conditions.

Whilst some people had leprosy through contamination with others, there are those who experienced being leprous through rebellion. They were in fact, cursed by God for disobeying His Word. When we neglect to obey Jehovah God who sees our works we are in a state of rebellion. Leprosy is figuratively used to denote sin. When we are in disobedience before God, we are depicted as leprous and like the lepers that became outcasts, we become unclean. The conscience state of our being makes one feel "removed" from the presence of God until we confess and are made clean through repentance. God cannot look at our sin except through His Son Jesus who is the eternal mediator for mankind. In fact, the only way God deals with us is through our Lord standing in the gap pleading before Him on our behalf. *"My little children, I am writing these things to you so that you may not sin. But if anyone does sin we have an Advocate, with Father, Jesus Christ the righteous" (1 John 2:1, ESV).*

2.3   Disobedience is Sin

To disrespect the Word of God is to give an entrance to sin. Adam and Eve brought sin into the human race and sadly, that pattern of behaviour, the inclination to test the boundaries of God's love is inherent in man. The flawed make-up of man, with an inherent predisposition to sin has been passed on through the spiritual gene pool. Like a naughty self-willed child, we love to disobey God. In fact, it is more a case of not having the strength in ourselves to overcome the powers of evil, so, we are easily defeated by Satan. Our strength to resist the evil one is secured in a loving obedient relationship with Jesus Christ. It would appear that our human nature is tended towards asserting our self-will when eternal choices are to be made.

Below, reference is drawn to three accounts in the Old Testament of sin bringing immediate consequences. The point being made is that spiritual disobedience brings consequences. In the first account, in (2 Kings 7: 3-10), King Uzziah became leprous because he dared to challenge whether the priests should have the exclusive right to offer incense.

The second case is that of Gehazi, the servant of Elisha who became leprous because he disobeyed the instructions given by God to his master. (2 Kings 5:20-27). Naaman, as mentioned above was a Syrian commander who had leprosy. On hearing of Elisha, he took leave of his duties and went to the prophet for prayer. After his healing, Naaman in thankfulness sought to lavish the prophet with gifts. However, instructed by God not to take anything from Naaman, Elisha told Gehazi he was forbidden to accept any gifts from Naaman. On his way home, Naaman was pursued by Gehazi who determined in his heart to take to himself some of the gifts. Naaman pulled up the carriage to see what the matter concerned. Gehazi conceived a lie in his heart to disobey the prophet in order to receive the gifts that Naaman had initially offered to the prophet Elisha.

Sometimes our folly, lifestyle, and even habits can lead to self-inflicted curses resulting in sickness and even death. Still, we know that God is merciful and His Spirit continues to urge us to repent when we fall short.

Another case of leprosy recorded is that of Miriam, Aaron's sister. Miriam and Aaron opposed Moses' leadership. In a pillar of cloud, God came down at the door of the tent and summoned Miriam and Aaron to come out. God spoke highly of His servant Moses and made known His indignation towards Miriam and Aaron's folly, (Numbers 12:10-15). The pair of them incensed that only Moses should be hearing from God incurred His wrath. He made an example of Miriam for disrespecting and challenging Moses' leadership.

Miriam was immediately afflicted with leprosy. It was Aaron who sought to intervene on the behalf of Miriam, imploring Moses to pray that the curse be staved off her. Now, we see that God drew reference to the requirements of the written law for her to be put away from the community. God did not make an exception for Miriam as He instructed that she be put outside of the camp for seven days of purification. She was required to go to the priest like any other person after that time to be certified clean. It must have been humiliating for her but justifiably so because she usurped her position.

2.4   The Power of the Word

It was the duty of the priest to ensure that those deemed unclean remained isolated for the duration of the time stipulated. In the New Testament, we see the leper who came to Jesus was healed, and Jesus told him to go to the priest. Here, we see Jesus abiding by the law's requirements. The man, although healed had to get a certificate showing that he was cleansed before being reintroduced into the community.

The power of the Word to heal the sick is what the ministry of Jesus was about. The above account is yet another example of Jesus being Lord over the works of affliction and sickness. The healing of the leper would be for the glory of God.

All powers of captivity are subject to the Word of God. Anything that is spiritually bound or tied can be loosed by the power of the cross. Jesus is referred to as the Word because when He speaks, the spirit behind the captivity is routed to roam in dry uninhabitable places, *"When an impure spirit comes out of a person, it goes through arid places seeking rest and does not find it. Then it says, 'I will return to the house I left"(Luke 11:24, NIV).* These spirits are driven from their comfortable abode in the souls of captive men. The unclean spirit is responsible for unsettling the people causing them to be sick and incapacitated. They are compelled to obey the authoritative Word of God and vacate the distressed soul. It is a complete work of grace that ministers to the whole person in mind, body, spirit, and soul. Those who were chained to their sins, unable to help themselves are released in the Potentate Name of our Lord. In acknowledgement of His Lordship and His power over the works of evil, these liberated folks run with the Good News declaring Jesus as Lord.

2.5   Spiritually Cleansed

The Greek translation 'katharizo' (Strong's 2511) means to make ceremonially clean. It is to be made pure. Under the law, the steps in place to deal with those who were diseased or those who were deemed social outcasts precipitated the action of the priest for the safety of all.

Jesus is the Chief of the Priesthood, and He did away with the traditions and ceremonies to bring about a new order for the healing of the people. His earthly ministry made it possible for rejected, hurting, and dispirited people to be spiritually uplifted, healed, and made whole. Jesus ministered to the whole person. In His role as Priest, He cared enough to make a difference. A new quality of life brought many benefits to the sick not least to be physically able to work and earn a living. Many impotent folks were delivered, eliminating any further need to be depending on others for meagre handouts.

Through the authority in the name of Jesus, all kingdoms and realms are subject to His rule. Mankind can, therefore, be made spiritually pure by the cleansing of His Word. Under the law, a blood sacrifice of animals was required for sins. Jesus' blood was the perfect atonement for sin that purifies sinful man enabling us to be drawn into fellowship and love with the Father of creation.

He is our Great High Priest and just as the earthly priests were required to assist the people in their healing and wellbeing, so did Jesus service their needs. He aids us and once we have been spiritually cleansed, as the lepers, we can again participate fully in the service of God. God sent His Word to heal us and to rescue us from every pit of destruction we can find ourselves in *(Psalms 107:20)*. Truly, we can be delivered from sin and renewed in the things of God. It is a joy to experience a loving relationship with God, but it is only possible when we forsake a wayward course.

2.6   Destined for God's Glory

I have no reservation in believing that the recorded cases of those who were healed by Jesus in the Scriptures were purposed to meet Him from the beginning of time. Their conditions had become chronic and beyond human help. Their only hope was in Jesus, the Healer and therefore, their cases were for the glory of God. Many were desperately sick, long-term disabled, dying or deceased. It is without a doubt that for many, their chances in life were impaired and who cared?

The demon possessed man and those in similar situations were socially banished from their families and communities living transiently among the tombs. *(1) "They went across the lake to the region of the Gerasenes. (2) When Jesus got out of the boat, a man with an impure spirit came from the tombs to meet him. (3) This man lived in the tombs, and no one could bind him anymore, not even with a chain. (4) For he had often been chained hand and foot, but he tore the chains apart and broke the irons on his feet. No one was strong enough to subdue him. (5) Night and day among the tombs and in the hills he would cry out and cut himself with stones. (6) When he saw Jesus from a distance, he ran and fell on his knees in front of him. (7) He shouted at the top of his voice, 'What do you want with me, Jesus, Son of the Most High God? In God's name don't torture me!' (8) For Jesus had said to him, "Come out of this man, you impure spirit!" (9) Then Jesus asked him, 'What is your name?'. 'My name is Legion,' he replied, 'for we are many.' (10) And he begged Jesus again and again not to send them out of the area" (Mark 1:1-10, NIV).*

As narrated in the verses above, the man was under a bond of wickedness. It was a 7-fold demonic occupation. The strength of the legions of demons caused him to react extremely violently. The local people feared walking pass the tombs. His reaction to others further perpetuated his loneliness and social rejection. It is a vicious cycle of fear and confusion causing mental and social retardation.

It is the intention of the enemy to isolate people in their suffering compounding their sense of inner anguish and fear. He was not in a balanced state emotionally, and the demons voluntarily spoke out of him. It is without a doubt, that demonic possession changes the personality of the person possessed because they are not acting of themselves in a right frame of mind. They live each day, in total confusion. The Devil is the originator of confusion and his spirit is impure removing its victim to a spiritually isolated abyss. Unless the greater power of the cross intervenes, it is by far a hopeless dilemma. *"For God gave us a spirit not of fear but of power and love and self-control." (2 Timothy 1:7, ESV).* Fear and torment are from the evil one and Jesus showed that God's power of love is conducive to possessing a sound, balanced and disciplined mind.

After Jesus had expelled the legions of demons, we see in verse 15 that the state of this young man was completely reversed. *(15) "And they came to Jesus and saw the demon-possessed man, the one who had had the legion, sitting here, clothed and in his right mind..." (Mark 5:15, ESV).* His peace was restored and his fragmented mind healed. It is only the blood of Jesus that can transform a broken life. Jesus urged him to go home to his community so that they could bear witness to the transforming power of God over the works of evil. When we are delivered from our circumstances we must bear witness through our testimony of faith so that others can believe on the Lord Jesus and come to know Him as their Lord.

2.7   A Fragmented Personality

There are a few perspectives on mental illness and demonic possessions. I refrain from giving an opinion except that from a biblical perspective, I believe the Scriptures as they are stated that Jesus can heal when there is no other hope. Staying with the case of the demonic man in section 2.6, the Scriptures illustrate that he lived in the place of departed souls. His physical situation paralleled his spiritual state. He was spiritually dead having been taken over by a legion of territorial spirits—about 5000 strong evil spirits. How he came to be in that state, we will never know. It is clear, however, that he was mercilessly tormented and his personality oscillated between glimpses of the real self and the possessed self. How do we know that? Well, when he saw Jesus, he began to cry for help as he ran towards Jesus. I am convinced that his feeble steps towards Jesus were the steps of faith needed for his deliverance. That one action was from him, the real self. He was desperately in need of help. Hence, his bouts of frustration and violence leading to self-harm were all attention-seeking signs.

However, based on my research on mental health, this man would possibly be labeled as having "manic depressive psychosis associated with demonic possession." As a layperson in mental illness classification, I could still yet be wrong. However, that is not the point I am bringing here. When the young man cried out "Son of the Most High God," it was the demons speaking out of him. When you read the full account, Jesus spoke in the singular and He also indicated plurally, perhaps, to the victim that he was a person in his own right separate from the demonic cohort.

When Jesus came upon the situation, the spirit realm became active. His presence would have disturbed the comfortable demons. They knew it was time to go because when Jesus comes, the tempter's power is broken. They cease to be in control of that habitat. The territory is taken over by the greater power. Demons are unwilling to leave their residence to roam in dry places. *"When an impure spirit comes out of a person, it goes through arid places seeking rest and does not find it. Then it says, 'I will return to the house I left." (Luke 11:24, NIV)*. They implored that Jesus send them into the herd of pigs. These spirits were unclean spirits, and they needed a host body to live in so they determined that the pigs would make a reasonable substitute.

Had it not been predetermined by God in eternity that His Son, Jesus should pass along the route others feared, that it is without a doubt that this beautiful soul would have been perpetually lost. *"Forasmuch then as the children are partakers of flesh and blood, He also himself likewise took part of the same, that through death he might destroy him that had the power of death, that is, the devil. And deliver them who through fear of death were all their lifetime subject to bondage" (Hebrews 2:14-15 ESV).*

Divine intervention in his situation is all that was required. The Healer of the people passing by would destroy the dark works of the evil spirits fully occupying the soul. They were routed into the unfortunate pigs leisurely grazing on the hillside. So numerous and violent were these evil forces coming out of the man that they forcibly entered the pigs hurling them down the steep slopes into the watery abyss.

The demons would have eventually destroyed the young man. *"The thief comes only to steal and kill and destroy. I came that they may have life and have it abundantly." (John 10:10, ESV).* When we are snatched from the hands of God through sin, purposes and destinies are destroyed. Spiritually, when we are in our right minds, spirit controlled, we can be powerful deterrents against evil. The fight is ultimately against Jesus but we are his hands and feet in the earth and the enemy desires that we all fail miserably. The fragmented personality of individuals can be restored to normalcy because the young man went on to become a faithful advocate of the power of the cross over the works of evil.

2.8 Broken Wasted Lives

The transient community of people without help is prevalent today. It is no different from Jesus' time. There are many people living on the fringes of their society, poor and dejected, without a home, or any quality of life and future. They are bound in 'grave clothes' of poverty, addictions to drugs, alcoholism, sexual sins, and many other areas of human deprivation and misery. *Jehovah-Roi* is the God who sees us just where we have fallen, helpless and alone. It is a spiritual problem so we are unable to help ourselves and recover from our brokenness without divine assistance.

Jesus told Judas Iscariot that the poor would always be around when he begrudgingly quibbled about the wasteful gesture of Mary as she lavished her devotion with the expensive ointment at Jesus' feet. Truly, truly it is so even today. The waste of human life is evident around us. It is indeed a human tragedy. Now, if Judas really had concern about the poor, there would be many opportunities for him to step up and help them. But we can deduce that he had no interest in the poor whatsoever, but rather, revealed the true intent of his heart and his preoccupation with money that became his undoing.

2.9   At the Feet of Jesus

It is official, there is healing at the feet of Jesus. *"Then great multitudes came to Him, having with them the lame, blind, mute, maimed, and many others; and they laid them down at Jesus' feet, and He healed them" (Matthew 15:30, ESV).* As I read the accounts of Jesus healing the people it dawned upon me that many fell at the feet of our Lord and worshipped Him. Healing is procured at the feet of Jesus. The blood that flowed from His feet at the cross is still flowing today for the healing of the nations. There is no greater place to be than at the feet of Jesus.

His earthly ministry would usher in the times of refreshing by the Word. The glory of the Son of God reached into the unreachable areas of human life. All that remained under strong demonic control was exposed and the veil of darkness torn away to reveal the miserable, abysmal and degenerate state of human lives under sin. *"And the whole multitude sought to touch Him, for power went out from Him and healed them all" (Luke 6:19, ESV).* The people were drawn into His presence and fell at His feet. It was the power of the cross that exposed human suffering and the level of spiritual deprivation. With compassion, He tended to their many diverse needs.

2.10   The State of the Heart

With the heart, we believe that Jesus is Lord and with the confession of our mouths we are saved. The people knew Jesus to be the Healer as they made their way by faith to secure their healing. It was a community effort to ensure the sick were brought to Jesus. Great crowds would gather to see Jesus' signs, miracles, and wonders. It was a cause for concern amongst the authorities and those who objected to the sick being healed, particularly on the Sabbath day were not spiritually informed that Jesus is our Lord of the Sabbath.

As the one found worthy to become the Deliverer of the people, the eternal priesthood was conferred upon the Son of God. As said earlier, the priesthood was an eternal office given after the order of Melchisedek who had no beginning or end of days. Likewise, Jesus has no beginning or end, but He was eternal in the heavens. In the order of remit, like the earthly priest, He would minister to the needs of the people. His ministry brought the sick, the cripple, the poor, and needy from outside the city gates of Jerusalem into the spiritual enclosures of His kingdom, the "new" Jerusalem.

In His kingdom, there are no "outsiders." He respects no one above another person; the high are made low and the low are lifted up. There is no gender difference with Jesus. In fact, women were ardent followers of His ministry. It was Mary Magdalene who was first at the tomb on His resurrection morning. It is without doubt, that many contemporary ministries exist because of faithful women. They are quietly behind the scenes in the "engine rooms" of ministries as passionate worshippers and prayer warriors. Their efforts may go unnoticed by those around them, but it is God who judges the heart. The Scriptures indicate that He will not judge by physical eyes as humankind but His perfect sight, through the seven eyes of the Spirit sees everything. Jesus endeared Himself to many women who would otherwise be viewed from the sidelines or pale into insignificance.

There are many "*Mary Magdalenes*" today. Women, emerging on the scene that have been brought to the forefront by God. They will be favoured to play significantly active roles in the end-time culminating of the church age. In fact, we will see this trend of women "breaking through" the spiritually fastened ceilings in churches, governments and other entities perversely dominated by men through the ages. I believe women have amenable hearts that God loves and many will be strategically positioned in the end-time work in the Body of Christ. To hold such positions in these spiritually challenging times will single one out for unprecedented attacks and ill treatment by those who have not the heart of Christ. Many have to stand alone in ministries because the enemy has made shipwreck of their lives for the gospel's sake.

In bible times, the cities were fortified entities, and it was the duty of the posted watchmen to keep guard of who entered and went out of the compound. The cross that Jesus hung from was posted outside of the city on Golgotha's hillside. During the tenure of His ministry, Jesus resorted to healing the people who were put outside of the city of Jerusalem. The people's hearts were receptive, and they sought Him out wherever He went into surrounding regions and nations. They were the needy followers of His divine works.

In life and in death, Jesus was an outcast. Hence, the Scriptures refer to His suffering outside the gate. Jesus suffered physically, emotionally, socially, spiritually—always coming under attack from the evil one. His life was epitomised by suffering and rejection during the time that He was here on the earth by the people He came to save. He was chosen over Barabbas to be crucified as they hailed Him, *"He said He is King of the Jews."*

2.11   Muzzling the Ox

The Jews were termed the "lost" house of Israel. It was for them first that Jesus came to bring salvation but their hearts were turned against Him. The Scribes, Pharisees, and other religious sects sought to entrap Him in the understanding of the law. The political rulers were under pressure to figuratively "muzzle the ox" because His speeches condemned them. The people loved Him and sought to be in His presence to hear His parables. *"And they were astonished at his teaching, for he taught them as one who had authority, and not as the scribes" (Mark 1:22, ESV).* The Word of God cut into the conscience of those who opposed Him as they sought to do Him evil. His verbal responses to their questionings were a continued source of irritation. They tried to inveigle Him into legal discourses pertaining to the interpretation of the law in order to trap Him on a technicality. It would serve to score them a victory over Him. Yet, for all that, Jesus continued to heal the people as He moved around the countryside of the regions bringing hope to those unable to help themselves. For the duration of His ministry, it was mainly the grateful Gentiles who would seek Him out.

2.12　A New Order

As Jesus came into His earthly ministry, He ushered in something fresh and new. It incited the people and caused a chatter to reverberate in the cities and hill countries. It was disturbing to the authorities, and their vain attempt at squashing it failed to abate the enthusiasm of the people, as they became grateful recipients of the work of grace. The powers of the leaders could not control this new movement.

Jesus went against the grain of the old order of life and society seeking the spiritually lost, sick and those in need of a physician. His intervention in human society was ultimately to set up His kingdom in the hearts of the people. When confronted by those who were religious, He said of Himself that He came not for the righteous, referring to the Pharisees, Scribes, and other sects, but for those who needed help. Those who criticised Him for healing the sick on a Sabbath were rebuked as not needing a healer. When the leaders were unable to stop Jesus, they sought to intimidate the people by employing subversive tactics. They reminded the people of the time when they could be healed but not on the Sabbath. *"Indignant because Jesus had healed on the Sabbath, the synagogue leader said to the people, 'There are six days for work. So come and be healed on those days, not on the Sabbath'"* (Luke 13:14,NIV).

Jesus is often referred to as the Great Physician and He always sought to rescind any arguments the leaders brought to Him against healing on a Sabbath day. He knew their hearts and even before they spoke, He preempted their carnal reasoning.

Behind the opposition to His ministry was the orchestrated plan of Satan to counter the works of grace. Satan used those hearts that

34

were made available as an entry point to advance his kingdom of darkness. At every opportunity, the enemy sought to discredit Jesus. He was often charged for things He did not do. He was accused of socialising with tax collectors. The inference being that he was not an honest person. He was supposed to be a friend of prostitutes implying that He made use of their services. He was portrayed as a winebibber or drunkard. *"The Son of Man came eating and drinking, and they say, 'Behold, a gluttonous man and a drunkard, a friend of tax collectors and sinners!' Yet wisdom is vindicated by her deeds" (Matthew 11:19, NASB).*

PART THREE
THE OPPOSITION

"For we wrestle not against flesh and blood but against principalities, powers and the rulers of the darkness of this world and wickedness in high places."

(Ephesians 6:12)

3.1   The Curse of Sin

The narrative recorded in the book of Matthew pertaining to the entrance of Jesus into our earthly realm reveals the spiritual resistance to abort the plan of God. This pattern of spiritual interference continues throughout the earthly life of our Lord. His ministry was constantly under attack by those used of the devil.

Jesus stepped into a spiritually dark world. As the Saviour of mankind, His mandate was to bring the glorious light that would illuminate in the dark recesses of the hearts of the people. The law of righteousness would rule over the law of sin. The law was introduced by God to keep men in His will. It sets the boundaries of our human coexistence with God and within human society. When we are in the will of God, we are free from the rule of unrighteousness or sin. We will give respect to God and humankind.

The spirit that opposed Jesus' entry into the world is still prevalent today to disrupt the advancement of the kingdom of righteousness in the hearts of the people. For example, the Devil used Herod in a murderous rage to seek and find the baby Jesus in order to destroy Him. That spiritually murderous Moloch spirit has reared its ugly head and heightened its activities as a global "ring of fire" around the children of God in Christian communities today. But there are many believers who will stand stoically to denounce the evil of the day and love Jesus as their Lord. There is no earthly power initiated by the kingdom of darkness that can forbid the advancement of God's kingdom in the earth. The power and authority we have in the name of Jesus are sufficient to combat the evil of the day. We have only to be connected to the source of our power, Jesus our Lord.

3.2   An Evil Remit

Satan had a mandate to obstruct the work of salvation and healing. That was the strength of the curse of sin. The epistle of Paul to the church at Ephesus reminded them of the bondage that comes from Satan, and Christ's power over his works. *"Even when we were dead in our trespasses, made us alive together with Christ—by grace you have been saved" (Ephesians 2: 5,6, ESV).* Whilst some of the people were under the bondage of religion, others were sick and under the bondage of affliction. It is without a doubt, that sin is a precursor to sickness and spiritual death. *"And you hath he quickened, who were dead in trespasses and sins"(Ephesians 2:1,KJV).* In principle, the affliction of the whole man is a result of sin from the fall of Adam. It is perhaps not untoward to advocate that ultimately, sickness and the deterioration of all entities of human life are rooted in the spiritual death that came through disobedience in the Garden of Eden.

Jesus showed through the Scriptures that He initially deals with the source of the problem that is the spirit behind the situation. He commands the unclean spirit to leave the people. *"When Jesus saw that a crowd was rapidly gathering, He rebuked the unclean spirit, saying to it, 'You deaf and mute spirit, I command you, come out of him and do not enter him again'" (Mark 9:25, ASV).* He then commands healing. The unclean spirits are the underlying cause of their oppression, torment, and pain. The cause and effects of sin are ruinous and debilitating causing people to feel trapped and hopeless in their situation. Those who made their way to Jesus had no other course of intervention to be made whole. Jesus was their last and only resort.

Not only did Jesus heal, but He also raised the dead to life. Lazarus was four days in the grave when his sister, to paraphrase said "Jesus you have come too late by now Lazarus has deteriorated and stinks." Jesus unperturbed brings calm to the troubled soul of His friends. According to the scriptures, Jesus is the firstfruit of those who have died. *"That the Christ must suffer and that, by being the first to rise from the dead, he would proclaim light both to our people and to the Gentiles" (Acts 26:23, ESV).* This refers to Jesus as the risen Lord who burst forth from the grave taking dominion over Satan's power over hell, death and the grave over mankind. *"Since then the children are sharers in flesh and blood, he also himself in like manner partook of the same; that through death he might bring to nought him that had the power of death, that is, the devil; and might deliver all them who through fear of death were all their lifetime subject to bondage" Hebrews 2:14-15, ASV).* Jesus broke the cords of spiritual death that held us in eternal captivity to sin. No longer are we bound by Satan's power, unable to be free from his tenacious clutches.

3.3   The Kingdom of Darkness

In order to bring understanding to the level of rejection experienced by Jesus against setting up His reign in men's hearts, one must look at the facts concerning the kingdom that has juxtaposed itself against the kingdom of God.

Satan is the Prince of Darkness and also the Prince of the power of the air. Because Satan is a spirit, he reigns in an invisible realm over the earth realm and also has the freedom to roam the earth seeking vacant hearts to reign in. *"In which you used to live when you followed the ways of this world and of the ruler of the kingdom of the air, the spirit who is now at work in those who are disobedient" (Ephesians 2:2, NIV).* As stated in Luke 4:6, the power Satan speaks of when he said to Jesus that he would give Him all the kingdoms of the world if He worshipped him is not his to give away. *"To you I will give all this authority and their glory, for it has been delivered to me, and I give it to whom I will."* He has no power of himself except that given by God. He is, therefore, ruling the airways for a short time. Satan is the author of lies. They originate from the personification of evil.

All power belongs to God and He gave that power to Jesus His Son. When Jesus was speaking to His disciples He said, *"... All authority in heaven and on earth has been given to me" (Matthew 28:18, ESV).* Jesus is sharing it with the saints as joint-heirs to His kingdom. Satan has no other power except that which he has taken illegally by organising a rebellion against God through the world system. He was here offering power to Jesus because he wanted Him to worship him. Imagine, Satan seeking to collude with Jesus to show utter contempt towards God. Satan presumptuously tempts the Son of God. It is no wonder that so many people are being overtaken easily as prey and deceived by Satan to join his orchestrated rebellion against God in the earth. Satan is rebuked and put in his place by Jesus when he is reminded that only God is worthy of worship. *"Then Jesus said to him, 'Be gone, Satan.' For it is written, "You shall worship the Lord your God and him only shall you serve'" (Matthew 4:10, ESV).*

The term "kingdom of darkness" sheds light on the covert operation of evil. The dark and hidden works of sin exemplify the order of Satan's rule. *"He has delivered us from the domain of darkness and transferred us to the kingdom of his beloved Son" (Colossians 1:13, ESV).* It is the exact opposite of Jesus' glorious work of grace that radiates in the hearts of those who will give entrance to the Word. The world is in a state of spiritual captivity, hence, Jesus came to rescue man from the iron grip of sin. So tenacious is the hold that only the power of God can break every chain. *"For he has rescued us from the dominion of darkness and brought us into the kingdom of the Son he loves" (Colossians 1:13).* The darkness refers to spiritual blindness in that outside of Jesus, man cannot see the depth of bondage that holds them in spiritual ignorance.

The Scripture advocates the *4-fold mandate* of Jesus' mission of salvation, deliverance, and healing. *"...to open their eyes and turn them from darkness to light, and from the power of Satan to God, so that they may receive forgiveness of sins and a place among those who are sanctified by faith in me"(Acts 26:18, NIV).* Clearly put, it is to:

- open the eyes of the spiritually blind

- transfer the power that holds mankind back to the Father

- enable men to receive God's forgiveness for sin

- be counted worthy of the faith with Christ Jesus

When we are in our sins we are biblically termed as being in "Egypt." When Jesus was a young child, His father, Joseph, was warned in a dream to flee down to Egypt to escape Herod's wrath. He quickly heeded the warning and took Jesus and His mother to Egypt distancing them from Herod's death trawl. It was during His time in Egypt growing into manhood that Jesus was prepared for His ministry. The time came when He was called out of Egypt to fulfill His spiritual mission as prophesied. *"...and remained there until the death of Herod. This was to fulfill what the Lord had spoken by the prophet, "Out of Egypt I called my son" (Matthew 2:13-15, ESV).* Egypt was a foreign land and His call out of Egypt is, therefore, symbolic of our escape from the worldly lure of sin into the kingdom of His light.

3.4   Spiritual Darkness

Jesus came into our world to open the spiritual eyes of the people so that they could understand through God's Word, the great deception leveled at mankind through the works of darkness. The Scriptures say that we must have no association with the works of darkness. *"Have nothing to do with the fruitless deeds of darkness, but rather expose them" (Ephesians 5:11, NIV).* Galatians 3 records that Jesus' death on the cross ultimately made an open shame of sin. The works of darkness were nailed to the cross exposing everything that was eternally hidden. Darkness dissipates under the illuminating works of grace.

The spiritual climate of this age epitomises dense darkness. The people are in a deeply lethargic state of spiritual sleep. There is no inclination in them to fight back and be aroused from a state of stupor. The spiritual fight or flight response to sense danger is inactive. Even though we are experiencing the fulfillment of the Scriptures and all evidence is directing man to the impending rapture, there appears to be no spiritual alertness to escape what is inevitable. It is a spiritual sleep and a spiritual response is required to awaken men out of sleep.

3.5   Disowned and Rejected

Jesus' rejection was of evil intent orchestrated by Satan. Satan uses people to carry out his will in the earth. Those whose hearts are opened to his influence of evil are mere puppets, and they are easily preyed upon.

It is thought that the Jewish religious leaders feared Jesus because He was bringing about change through His message of hope. They were comfortable in their abode of spiritual darkness and the brilliance of Jesus' light was intimidating. Change is never welcome by people, as history has shown us that global and national conflicts usually arise out of change. Change can be chaotic, uncomfortable and it usually causes people to respond by resisting it. Resistance comes to changes in family life, in church leadership, in new practices in the workplace or governmental changes. The concept of change requires people to shift in their mental and emotional construct. That is the fundamental angst with change. People do not like to shift from within themselves unless it is self-directed. When change comes from outside of us, it affects the internal working of our construct. To accommodate external influences and change, we have to start the process from within. Acceptance that you cannot influence the external process of change is the initial stage of moving on.

Change is a progressive process, and we must resign ourselves to the inevitable outcomes that will result from change. In most situations we only have control over our internal construct to ensure we embrace change positively to avoid a negative primal response. The religious leaders were not willing to look within themselves and accept a new pattern of thinking and understanding. It was a spiritually inherent problem with this cohort. The person who could spiritually help them was resisted and His ministry rejected. They wanted to secure their way of life that was prosperous under the political rule. It was never about the healing and welfare of the people. It was always about their position and status before the people. The spirit in leadership that resists change is a foundational spirit and it is still with us today.

At the beginning of Jesus' earthly life, we see Him proclaimed "King of the Jews" by astrologers seeking to find Him. *"Where is He that is born King of the Jews?" (Matthew 2:2,ASV).* At the cross, the people mocked Him yet unwittingly they declared Him to be "King of the Jews." Even an inscription was contemptuously placed above His head but it served to declare His Lordship, "This is Jesus the King of the Jews." The Word declares that everything in creation pays homage to the King of kings and Lord of lords. Even those who with feigned lips shall bow and worship Him as King of the nations.

3.6   Out with the Old!

Jesus was considered an outsider, a loner and misunderstood amongst the religious peers. He conducted His ministry outside of the mainstream groups, effortlessly injecting new life into old practices. From His enemy's perspective, there could not be anything more irritating than a new *"upstart"* emerging on the scene making a great difference in the lives of the people.

We all know that there are more similarities amongst people than there are differences. Ironically, it is always one's differences that cause anger and envy amongst competitors. The opponents were incensed with envy and everywhere Jesus went, they were on His heel. They criticised Him, questioning His authority and wherever possible, they sought to ensnare Him by His Word. It is always the Word that comes under attack, it is not intended towards the people who are the bearers of the Good News although they do suffer for the call. Jesus is the Word, a formidable buffer against Satan's attack. The servant of God only feel the aftershock of a spiritual impact, yet, it can be so painful.

The religious leaders were obstructive against the new movement and the good deeds being done to the people. They were undoubtedly acting as informants to the political authorities spreading lies. They sought to destroy Jesus because He dared to declare Himself as the Son of God, the Sent One and the one who has the power to forgive sins.

Those who contended with Jesus were not for Him or His purpose to heal and deliver the people from spiritual oppression. In effect, they were alienating themselves from the Promise by refusing to agree with Jesus on matters pertaining to the application of the law. They missed the point that Jesus was the fulfillment of the Scriptures and therefore, the law of righteousness was the surpassing glory of the law written on tablets of stone. The old order could no longer suffice in delivering the people from their bondage and oppression. The interpretation of the law was long without efficacy. It was convoluted and without the power to keep the people from the burden of sin.

3.7 Emerging on the Scene

There is no doubt that Jesus' ministry caused His opponents to be intimidated and aroused by fear, they sought to frustrate His work. In the time of Jesus, religion and state matters were co-essential elements of the way of life. As with any society, however basic, religion, the law, and politics are integral constituted tenets for human organisation.

The political leaders had a great sway in the religious order. Criticism and obstruction towards Jesus and His ministry to heal and restore the people came mainly from the leadership hierarchy of the society. There were those teachers who were weighed down by the legal interpretation of the law; as well as spiritual leaders tied to traditions, customs, and practices reinforced through repetitive observances. Then, we see that the religious groups were segregated by their doctrinal differences and persistently questioned Jesus' authority to do the things He did. Last, but by no means least, there were the political leaders intrigued and bewildered by the emergence of this new ministry of Jesus. They were concerned because it was written that He was the King of the Jews. His message of hope was exciting the people causing a stir and making them tetchy and nervous. They felt threatened by this supposedly "new" King of the Jews.

The prophetic anointing of Jesus would have no doubt stirred the atmosphere and all things hidden were being revealed. His authority exposed the true intent of the hearts of those who were in positions of authority to serve the people. They were not really for the people and the meager efforts at helping the poor, sick, and needy were by far inadequate and wholly ineffective. *"(45) Many of the Jews therefore, who had come with Mary and had seen what he did, (46) believed in him, but some of them went to the Pharisees and told them what Jesus had done. (47) So the chief priests and the Pharisees gathered the council and said, 'What are we to do? For this man performs many signs. (48) If we let him go on like this, everyone will believe in him, and the Romans will come and take away both our place and our nation.'" (John 11:45-48, ESV).*

3.8   Without Compassion

What can we deduce from the constant exchanges between Jesus and the high priests, religious leaders, Scribes, Pharisees, and Sadducees? They were all part of the religious and political cohort of the day. They differed in aspects of the interpretation of the law and matters concerning the resurrection of Jesus. What is certain is that they were against His ministry. It is clear that they did not carry the burden Jesus had for the people. Neither did they have the compassion that our Lord had for their healing and deliverance from unclean spirits. *"And when Jesus went out He saw a great multitude; and He was moved with compassion for them, and healed their sick" (Matthew 14:14, ESV).*

"By what authority do you do these things, they enquired.?"(Mark 11:27-28), The Pharisees were incensed with Jesus because they believed that He made light, the seriousness of the law as they interpreted it. They were blocked by ordinances and over-identification with the requirements of the law. Jesus' ease with the people made their religion appear empty. In essence, the law was burdensome to the people. The rigidity of the law was actually working against the people. For instance, they could not do anything on the Sabbath, and Jesus in comparison healed the people whenever they presented themselves with their needs. They were livid that He appeared to disobey the law, and they

sought to publicly censure His ministry. Jesus' love and compassion revealed their true motives, and they felt uncomfortable having Him around. The polarity of the two kingdoms causes the tension and is evidence that they cannot coexist in the same territory.

Since the authorities showed little concern for the people and the issues they faced on a daily basis, they came to Jesus with all manner of conditions desiring the Deliverer to make them whole. He came to set the captives free from all forms of bondage. This scripture highlights the range of needs before our Saviour. *Then great multitudes came to Him, having with them the lame, blind, mute, maimed, and many others; and they laid them down at Jesus' feet, and He healed them"(Matthew 15:30, ESV).*

PART FOUR

HOLISTIC HEALING

(13)"You made all the delicate, inner parts of my body and knit me together in my mother's womb. (14) Thank you for making me so wonderfully complex! Your workmanship is marvelous-- how well I know it. (15) You watched me as I was being formed in utter seclusion, as I was woven together in the dark of the womb. (16) You saw me before I was born. Every day of my life was recorded in your book. Every moment was laid out before a single day had passed. (17) How precious are your thoughts about me, O God. They cannot be numbered!

(Psalms 139:13-17, NLT)

4.1   The Whole Person

What is holistic healing? The *Merriam-Webster Dictionary* gives a simple definition for holistic as "relating to the whole system and not individual parts." Again, a simple explanation provided is "to become healthy and completely well again."

Holistic healing relates to the whole system. That is someone's physical, mental, spiritual, psychological and emotional well-being. When the whole person's needs are addressed, there is an improvement in their life chances and life conditions. In the treatment of illnesses, Western practitioners have tended to address the problem of individual's needs in an ad hoc fashion. The focus primarily deals with the problem hence, medicine is given to deal with specifics. The Eastern practitioners have long sought to deal with the systemic cause thereby focusing on the wider underlying root issues.

Eastern health practitioners have held the view that diseases and illnesses occur when the body is out of alignment. For over 6000 years, the Eastern practitioners have sought to align the body and bring about a balance using a range of herbal medicines and proven techniques to aid recovery and health in the whole body. Herbs are natural earth produces that are digested to improve the metabolic and other systems of the body that are weak and not functioning at an optimum. God intended that we use herbs for food and for healing. *"And to every beast of the earth, and to every bird of the heavens, and to everything that creeps on the earth, everything that has the breath of life, I have given every green plant for food" (Genesis 1:29, ESV).* Man is part of God's creation with the breath of life. In creation God placed herbs in the earth for man. Herbs are supplements and food that gives health and strength to the body. Understanding the benefits of herbs and super foods as beneficial to the body is important in order to dispel ignorance that can cause us to perish unnecessarily.

It is widely known that stress is thought to be a precursor to many ailments in the body. Stress is a major cause of systemic imbalances in the body. The body over time can become sluggish and acidic rather than active and alkaline. When the body is acidic, it creates the right conditions for diseases. An acidic body wears a *frown*. An alkaline body wears a *smile*.

4.2   Systemic Harmony

The equilibrium of the whole system in well-being is not a new concept, but rather, it is a biblical fact. A disposition of joy and positive emotions is healing. The mind and body are an integral whole bringing health. When we are in that state of harmony, the body releases a chemical compound located in the brain called dopamine. It revives the body and causes it to function at an optimum level by the transmission of positive nerve impulses. *"A cheerful heart is medicine but a crushed spirit dries up the bones" (Proverbs 1:22). "Gracious words are a honeycomb, sweet to the soul healing to the bones" (Proverbs 16:24).* Again, we are encouraged in the Scriptures to pay attention to our attitude towards others and to possess a kind spirit because they are positive healing properties.

The human constitution of cells, systems, chemistry profiles and all its functions forms a complex and unique structure. It is a skillfully engineered system of multifaceted parts forming an integrated whole. For the best and most favourable outcome to healthy living, the God who created us knows our frame, and He directs us to His Word that underpins all our efforts at good health. Indeed, the completeness of our healing is secured in salvation. Yes, we may still become sick in the body and mind, as the flesh is corruption and therefore subject to pain and decay. The scripture outlines that though the physical being perishes because of age and deterioration the inner man is renewed day by day. The Spirit of God keeps one fresh and renewed in their spirit man.

Many people seek to be made whole focusing only on the mind and body but the spirit man needs healing too. When all these elements of our being are in harmony with God's Word, we are at an optimum level of wholeness. Yet our wellbeing is only guaranteed when we have learnt to love others and ourselves as God loves us. Healing is deep and meaningful when it comes from the gracious act of forgiveness. It is a releasing action on the part of the offended and gets the attention of God. He responds when we seek to be healed at deeper levels of our being by letting go of those who have hurt us. It may seem hard, but it pays dividends in the long run and combats the harmful effects of stress.

4.3   The Whole Person

Clearly, we are looking here at a comprehensive approach to healing and wellbeing. A skilled practitioner will seek to understand the range of needs of an individual and exercise within their professional boundaries the necessary interventions needed to aid the process of healing. It is without a doubt that there are many contributory factors to illnesses necessitating a degree of professional understanding in order to provide the best possible treatment and cure.

It takes an empathic practitioner to draw on the best possible course of treatment. Often times, that level of service is not adequately given to an individual because of the range of care issues. With the best intent and purposes, helping the sick can fall short of what is understood to be a holistic remedial service.

The question was asked above, "What is holistic healing?" A standard dictionary definition was provided. It is, therefore, imperative that when it comes to understanding the depth of human needs, one has to consider not only the physical being but also the spiritual dimensions. I believe that the best place to commence is in the Word of God. The knowledge of God surpasses the intellect of man's wisdom. It was God who created man and since the beginning of time, His governance of all entities of human life has been faithfully coursed by His Word. From that premise, we can begin to learn about Jesus, the one who makes whole the mind, body, spirit and soul through His ministry of reconciliation.

Just listening to the Spirit can provide the answer to an ailment or chronic problem.

There are countless stories of people revealing that God told them to go and forgive an individual or group of people to be emotionally and spiritually released—even cases of what one should drink or eat in order to be cured of diseases. For me, God connected me to a Jewish woman who through her knowledge of health helped me to recover from the effects of dramatic and violent life changes that distressed my entire being. There are people with the heart that God can use in this season of worldwide healing and reconciliation. Help may not come from the channels you would expect so keep listening to the Spirit. When we do not have the answers, God cares enough to whisper the solution or point you in the right direction through people connections.

It is on the above point that I express that in this season of healing, God revealed to me that many areas of healing have been ignored because of ignorance. For instance, through the ministry of deliverance God has shown me that the territories of acupuncture, yoga, reflexology and other methods and techniques that Christians have dismissed should be considered and the ground of their philosophy renounced and declared hallowed unto God. Many of these disciplines have their roots in Eastern religions. The power that is in us is greater than that in the world. We can boldly cancel the prayers to gods and deities and begin to take back dominion over all entities of life.

The techniques, gifts and practices of people all belong to God. The earth is the Lord's and the fullness thereof, the worlds and they that dwell therein. Even the spirits behind the different areas of healing are subject to God. God created everything for His glory. He deserves the credit and the honour for all our arts, creativity and expressions. We have been given dominion in the earth and as Christians the authority to seize territories, bind the spirit operating in that territory has been given unto us. The kingdom of God has suffered violently coming under provocation and attacks. Those who are violent in taking back possession particularly in this season of Jubilee can have what they desire.

The benefits of healing techniques, practices, gifts and abilities are from God and we must take dominion. I boldy say we should seize the territories and declare them to be Christ-centred and for the glory of God.

There are many people that have practiced Reiki, yoga, meditation, acupuncture and other healing techniques and they are coming to salvation in this end time. It is not God's will that these skills become redundant but rather that they be used for His glory.

Initially these practitioners need to go through a deliverance process and thereby renounce the covenants they have entered into with the spirit behind the healing method. If they begin to use the scriptures and channel their technique through the Spirit of God many can benefit from these skills because God has given man the ability to do the things they do. The problem we are faced with for generations are spirit-borne. The enemy has manipulated and controlled many areas of human life. The great minds behind many practices and techniques are not Christ centred but we can begin to claim them for God.

4.4   The Complete Self

These are four distinct tenets that constitute the entirety of the human self. Although technically they could be condensed into three tenets as the mind is part of the soul. *"For the word of God is alive and active. Sharper than any double-edged sword, it penetrates even to dividing soul and spirit, joints and marrow; it judges the thoughts and attitudes of the heart"* *(Hebrews 4:12,NIV).*

A brief synopsis of each subject is provided.

- Spirit
- Mind
- Body
- Soul

4.4.1 The Spirit

Job 32:8 illustrates that *"There is a spirit in man, and the breath of the Almighty gives him understanding."* Through the spirit in us, we can gain wisdom from God, the font of all knowledge. Zechariah 12:1 confirms that God *"forms the spirit of man within him."* Again, in the New Testament, we see the apostle Paul attesting to man's mental abilities as being spirit initiated. *"For what man knows the things of a man except the spirit of the man which is in him?" (1 Corinthians 2:11, NKJV).* The spirit is an eternal part of our being and cannot be separated from God. We are inextricably connected to God through His Spirit abiding with us.

4.4.2 The Mind

The mind, as said earlier is essentially part of the soul, comprising our will, thoughts, and emotions. This aspect of our being forms our personality and the unique self. *"But you should put aside from you your first way of life, that old man, which is corrupted by deceitful desires, And you should be made new in the spirit of your minds. And you should put on the new man, who has been created by God in righteousness and in the purity of the truth" (Ephesians 4:22-24, Aramaic Bible).*

The mind is a complex matter formed of two states. Namely, the conscious and the sub-conscious states. It is in the conscious part of our being that the cognitive processing system comes into play enabling us to reason, think and understand. The subconscious, on the other hand, is the repertoire of our deep-seated beliefs, attitudes, emotions, memories and feelings. It is in these hidden intangible regions that we cannot fully comprehend who we are. It is God who holds us in the palm of His hand, and He knows the revealed and hidden aspects of our being.

4.4.3 The Body

The body is the only natural tenet. Hence, I believe it can be stated categorically that our human composite is more spiritual than physical. We are truly made in the image of God. The body belongs to the earth and is formed from the dust. *"Then the LORD God formed a man from the dust of the ground and breathed into his nostrils the breath of life, and the man became a living being" (Genesis 2:7, NIV).* The composite of our physical body has the chemical trace elements of the soil from the earth. This provides infallible proof of our physical make up. Hence, the phrase used at funerals 'dust to dust, ashes to ashes'. Man came from the dust and will return to the dust.

The body is a degradable matter, and the earth eventually claims its own. *"As for man, his days are like grass; he flourishes like a flower of the field; for the wind passes over it, and it is gone, and its place knows it no more." (Psalms 103:15-16).* The grass is used metaphorically to bring context to the finiteness of our humanity. Our life span is a "wisp of vapour" momentarily seen in the passage of time.

4.4.4 The Soul

"Thus also it is written: 'Adam the first man was a living soul; the last Adam - The Life Giver Spirit'" (1 Corinthians 15:45, Aramaic Bible). "And the Lord God formed man of the dust of the ground, and breathed into his nostrils the breath of life; and man became a living soul" (Genesis 2:7,NIV). The soul can be described as immortal although some writers differ in their understanding. The soul is the tangible or intangible matter of our human composite. The tangible matter can be touched or perceived through the senses. The inner being can be understood by what is communicated through verbal reasoning, expressions, and feelings. The intangible being is imperceptible matter that cannot be touched yet there is still a dynamic interface with the world by what is revealed from the subconscious.

The soul and the spirit are the essence of our humanity that is inseparable from God. We are a three-fold composite of body, spirit, and soul as the apostle Paul communicated to the church at Thessalonica. *"May God himself, the God of peace, sanctify you through and through, may your whole spirit, soul and body be kept blameless at the coming of our Lord Jesus Christ" (1 Thessalonians 5:23,NIV).* The soul of man never dies. It is separated from the body at death and remains in a transitory holding place until such time when God deals with the matter of our eternal abode.

As can be seen from the explanations provided above regarding the four areas of our being, in light of the Scriptures, we are made in the image of the eternal God. Therefore, when we are made whole through the Word of God, it encapsulates the whole of our being. God leaves nothing to chance. He is amazingly perfect in His understanding and continues to repair and heal our broken lives. *"Beloved, I wish above all things that thou mayest prosper and be in health, even as thy soul prospereth"(3 John 1:2, KJV).* There is no greater love than the love of the Father. As depicts a loving father with a child so is God to His people. He will succor you and bear you up in His loving arms when tender loving care is required.

4.5 A Spirit Behind The Problem

Throughout the Gospels, we see the dynamic, life-changing ministry of Jesus meeting the complete needs of individuals. Jesus' healing ministry addresses the heart of the matter. The teachers of the law were inquisitive to know how the blind man was cured. They enquired of Jesus whether it was him or his parents who sinned. Jesus said neither of them but that he was born like that for the glory of God. It was a case of the young man being blind from birth so it was perhaps a birth defect. Jesus proceeded to sit on the ground and make spittle from the soil to rub over his eyes. He then instructed the man to go and wash in the pool of Siloam, which is interpreted "sent" in Hebrew. You will note from these scriptures that in the case of this man, Jesus did not rebuke or cast out of him any demons.

Notably, in other accounts of His healing, Jesus deals with the spirit behind the problem or the sickness. He would rebuke the "unclean" spirit and that was enough to discharge them. He commanded them to come out and not to enter another person. Why would spirits be in the people tormenting them with sickness, disability, and mentally challenging issues? It is because of the inherent nature of sin. Sin is characterised by spiritual deterioration and death. Sin is a complete embodiment of what is evil and destructive. It has a grip on a human life and is holistically devastating.

4.6   The Cause and Effects of Sin

There is always a "cause and effect" behind a spiritually deprived life. The cause of a sinful life undoubtedly results from following the course of this world. The devil has dominion in the earth realm, and it is within his realm of power that people are brought under his influence to disobey God's Word of governance for their lives. One is drawn away from the presence of God into the sway of spiritual darkness. Of course, we do have free will in determining the choices we make. However, it comes with personal responsibility.

The "effects" of sin can be far reaching affecting ensuing generations because they have not been nurtured in the Word of God. It becomes a generational curse as families, communities, and nations live under the ancestral curses of their fore-parents. The generational propensity to err in that particular area of sin becomes an iniquity. It takes a greater power, the Word of God to command the spirits behind the problem to leave, to seize the power behind their activity and cast them out. Jesus has the authority to break the strongholds of sin from all areas of human life. Living outside of God's presence leaves one deprived of inner healing and the joy that comes through salvation. The end result of living a life outside of God's gift of salvation is to be eternally banished from the presence of God. When the cost of eternal separation from God is weighed against living by the world's standards it is spiritually sobering. Yet, it cannot be fully appreciated without the Spirit bringing conviction.

It is in effect a life wasted, and it leads to eternal destruction. The potential and heritage we can have through Jesus are denied us when we choose to remain outside of God's righteousness. So tenacious is the grip of sin that unless the greater power of God is employed to break the cycle of spiritual deprivation, the sin of iniquity continues unabated being passed down to ensuing generations.

4.7   A Greater Power

So effective was the ministry of Jesus that it caused the people to come out of their habitats and humble dwellings to seek His service. *"When the even was come, they brought unto him many that were possessed with devils: and he cast out the spirits with his word..." (Matthew 8:16, ESV).* What was on offer was spiritually different, life transforming and divinely empowering. The people were healed and restored to health in mind, body, spirit, and soul.

Jesus' touch was encompassing because He addressed not only their spiritual needs but also their social needs. He told the prostitute to go and sin no more. She was able to go on to live a productive life understanding her self-worth. The woman He met at the well left well-informed about who she is. A change in the lifestyle of this woman would probably have improved her ability to form platonically meaningful relationships. She ran to tell her village folks about the stranger at the well, "come and see," she said. Paraphrasing, she was actually saying. "Come and see a man at the well. He is a prophet, He can tell you all things about yourself." Many others ran with the Good News even though Jesus at times cautioned them not to say anything. Wisdom taught our Lord that His enemies would not be too enthused to hear of the good works He did on behalf of His Father. They were plotting to take Him down albeit not before His time.

4.8   Faith In The Giver

Throughout the Scriptures, it is clear that faith is a precursor to our healing. When Jesus saw the faith of the seekers it moved Him with compassion to meet their needs.

The Scriptures indicate that if we do not have faith in God, we can expect nothing from Him. (6) *"But let him ask in faith, with no doubting, for the one who doubts is like a wave of the sea that is driven and tossed by the wind· (7) For that person must not suppose that he will receive anything from the Lord" (James 1:6-7, ESV).*

Could it be that the reason why Jesus always seemed to comment on the faith of those who came to Him was because He wanted to emphasise the importance of faith in receiving our healing? *"Then Jesus answered and said to her, 'O woman, great is your faith! Let it be to you as you desire.' And her daughter was healed from that very hour" (Matthew 15:28, ESV).* When faith is exercised, it catches the attention of Jesus. It is like a magnet, and it draws on His strength. The power in Him is then released on the seeker. Again, in scripture, we see that the prayer of faith saves the sick. *"And the prayer of faith shall save the sick, and the Lord shall raise him up; and if he has committed sins, they shall be forgiven him" (James 5:15, KJV).* This indicates that when we pray for those who are sick, we must first believe that our Lord is able to deliver them from all bondage and affliction. So the servant of God must have faith in the Word to deliver the people from all bondage.

From the account of the Scriptures, everywhere Jesus went the people sought Him to be made whole. *"When evening had come, they brought to Him many who were demon-possessed. And He cast out the spirits with a word, and healed all who were sick, that it might be fulfilled which was spoken by Isaiah the prophet, saying, 'He Himself took our infirmities and bore our sicknesses'" (Matthew 8:16,17, ESV).* Faith in the Saviour caused them to come out of their hiding places and make their way to Him. Families and friends ensured that the sick were brought by whatever means, even on crude constructions and laid them at His feet. Jesus felt their pain, He saw their faith and responded with compassion.

When Jesus came across the crippled man at the pool of Bethesda he was a chronic case having been disabled for a long time. Jesus enquired as to whether he required healing? *"When Jesus saw him lying there and knew that he had already been there a long time, he said to him, 'Do you want to be healed?'"* *(John 5:6, ESV)*. It almost seems like an insensitive response, but Jesus is purposeful in His service to the people, and it must be reciprocated. It is imperative that we are active participants in our healing. Faith in Jesus' ability to restore our lives to health is an important factor, and we must be single-minded in procuring our deliverance.

There is no doubt that some people do not want to be healed. They have learnt to cope with disability and life infirmities to the point that there is resignation and acceptance of their state. Jesus knew that in some cases it would be so. Hence his question *'Do you want to be made whole?'* For some the changes that would come from being healed is a daunting prospect. For some it may be the fear of change bringing with it anxiety to have to adjust their lives for which they are not prepared to do so. The enemy brings unnecessary fear that keeps people entrenched in chronic situations. The reality is that they would be released from the captivities they are held in. As servants of God we too should ask people is they want to be healed because if they are not willing to exercise faith it is a pointless effort because there will be no healing. For those who desired healing they made their way to Jesus as His reputation as "the Healer" spread throughout the regions.

PART FIVE

JESUS IS LORD

Isaiah 53

He was despised and rejected by men;
A man of sorrows, and acquainted with grief;
And as one from whom men hide their faces
He was despised, and we esteemed him not.
Surely he has borne our griefs and carried our sorrows;
Yet we esteemed him stricken, smitten by God, and afflicted.
But he was pierced for our transgressions;
He was crushed for our iniquities;
Upon him was the chastisement that brought us peace,
And with his wounds we are healed.
And the Lord has laid on him the iniquity of us all.
He was oppressed, and he was afflicted,
And they made his grave with the wicked and
With a rich man in his death,
Although he had done no violence and
there was no deceit in his mouth.
And was numbered with the transgressors;
Yet he bore the sins of many and makes intercession for
the transgressors.

5.1　The Suffering Servant

The ambivalence towards Jesus was borne of evil intent. Even though His enemies saw the miracles, signs, and wonders, they could not entertain the idea of Him being the Son of God and able to forgive sins. He contradicted what they believed was written in the book of the Law. These ambiguities caused many of the doubters to feel contempt towards Him.

The prophecy of Him recorded in Isaiah 53 depicts a man laden with the sorrows of mankind, yet, He did not complain or seek to assert His will but with a spirit of humility, He bore the shame and rejection for the salvation and healing of the world.

During the time of His ministry, Jesus' manner at times appeared brusque and dismissive. He was greatly misunderstood. His personality and attitude may at times alienated Him from His religious peers but His heart was compassionate and caring towards those in need. Isaiah described the suffering servant as docile, unassuming and harmless. He was mute, not willing to make a case for Himself but remained passive under provocation and mistreatment. Isaiah's reference to Him as a sheep indicates that Jesus was as a lamb defenseless against the predatory forces lining the route on His way to His death. He was the Lamb of God who came to take away the sins of the world. Unassuming and harmless He fulfilled His divine purpose for mankind.

5.2　Holy and Anointed One

"And Jesus, full of the Holy Spirit, returned from the Jordan and was led by the Spirit in the wilderness" (Luke 4:1, ESV).

Jesus is the Holy and Anointed One who will pour out the end-time refreshing. It is a time of spiritual refreshing for the world. In Hebrew '*Malqosh*' means the "latter rain" or the last season of the year's rain (*Strong 4456*). Rain signifies abundance in the harvesting of the crops. Without rain, the crops would languish and become stunted in growth. Drought diminishes the joy and expectation of the people who look forward to a heavy yield from the harvest.

According to the Scriptures, the Gospel must be preached in the entire world. *"And this gospel of the kingdom will be proclaimed throughout the whole world as a testimony to all nations, and then the end will come" (Matthew 24:14, ESV).* Jesus will gather in the harvest of souls in the world. From the four corners of the globe, they will lift up the name of Jesus as the "pourer" who saturates us with the latter rain of the end-time outpouring as recorded by Joel 2:23.

If Jesus is the metaphor of a lamb, in a two-fold representation He is depicted as the Lion from Judah's tribe ferociously brutal and uncompromising to repel the foe. He came to break the chains of affliction and oppression and set up His kingdom on earth. Every bondage known to man is broken releasing the captives from their confinements. *"When evening had come, they brought to Him many who were demon-possessed. And He cast out the spirits with a word, and healed all who were sick, that it might be fulfilled which was spoken by Isaiah the prophet, saying, 'He Himself took our infirmities and bore our sicknesses'" (Matthew 8:16,17, KJV).*

5.3   A New Life

As we established earlier, the concept of reconciliation belongs to Jesus. He is the originator of the ministry of reconciliation. *(17) "Therefore, if anyone is in Christ, he is a new creature; the old things passed away; behold, new things have come. (18) Now all these things are from God, who reconciled us to Himself through Christ and gave us the ministry of reconciliation, (19) namely, that God was in Christ reconciling the world to Himself, not counting their trespasses against them, and He has committed to us the word of reconciliation..."(2 Corinthians 5:17-19, ESV).* Clearly, the Scriptures denote that it is through salvation that we receive the newness of life. We are ultimately and spiritually healed and restored to the things that God intended for mankind. Through our reconciling to God in the spirit, the ungodly works of hate, war, torment, and unhappiness are replaced by His love, peace, joy and godly contentment in Christ. These are righteous acts of grace poured upon those who will receive the Father's love.

If the spirit of man is made whole, then the effects to the body, mind, and soul are harmonious. These tenets of our being experience a balance that is healing. It is the quality of spiritually renewing vitality embodied in the being of a person. With the best intentions, we all seek to find that equilibrium in the whole being. Variance in our relationship with God came through sin. Mankind is now in a state of flux as the rapidity of life changes being experienced is having an adverse effect on the whole person. The whole creation is groaning under the curse of sin. *(18) "For I consider that the sufferings of this present time are not worth comparing with the glory that is to be revealed to us. (19) For the creation waits with eager longing for the revealing of the sons of God"* (Romans 8:18-19, ESV).

Contemporary living is characterised by chronic stress. It is now a way of life affecting even young children. It is a damning truth that people are now exposed to increased levels of stresses across their life cycle. It is the power of the cross that helps us to cope and overcome the problems life throws at us. The bible encourages us to be content in whatever state we find ourselves. Not always easy, I might add but we are admonished to rest in the hope of His promises. There is a refuge from the storm. In the cleft of the Rock our Lord is there as a safe retreat. We are safe in the hiding place found only in Jesus who feels the impact of all life's crises. We begin to live anew in Jesus Christ who takes away the pain so that we can be renewed in His enduring peace.

5.4   The Clarion Call

There is an expectation of something about to happen affecting the whole world. It is an intervention of God to shift the order of human life. I believe that we are about to experience an end-time outpouring of God's love and healing for mankind. Those in spiritual darkness will be willing in the day of His power. The unrestrained last days' power to release people in chronic and deep conditions from the demonic hold of sin is imminent. I believe that we are about to enter into *an unusual spiritually active 7-year period.* During that season, we will experience a euphoric state of spiritual restoration, reconciliation, and healing as never seen. It is being ushered in under the Spirit-led urging of forgiveness and reparation of personal and historical sins. Now is the time to confess and repent. Take heed to what the Spirit is saying. If you need to repent and do your first works over once again—do it! The first works are the contrition of sins followed by repentance and restitution. *"Let no debt remain outstanding, except the continuing debt to love one another, for whoever loves others has fulfilled the law" (Romans 13:8, NIV).* After this time of refreshing, I believe those who have not heeded the warning and received Jesus' grace will find themselves hardened to a dismal state of spiritual loss. It is a serious contemplation because it is this time of healing that will prepare one for the impending glorious rapture of the saints from the earth. It is **NOT** a fairy tale or fiction!

O-O-O-O-O-O-O

*I believe what God is saying to me is that everyone on the face of the earth must take heed and repent in this season **of euphoric outpouring of healing and salvation!!!** It is a short season of eternal grace given to mankind!!! Do NOT miss this end-time season to repent!!! The next 7 years will be intensely testing for Christians.*

I believe the joy and healing received during the next 7 year period will sustain us as we enter the tribulation period until God calls His people away. (16) "For the Lord himself will descend from heaven with a cry of command, with the voice of an archangel, and with the sound of the trumpet of God. (17) And the dead in Christ will rise first. Then we who are alive, who are left, will be caught up together with them in the clouds to meet the Lord in the air, and so we will always be with the Lord" (1 Thessalonians 4:16-17, ESV).

Those who endure the season of persecution will receive a crown of life for their faithfulness as the rapture of the saints takes place. The Bible says we will be taken out of the tribulation period. The Spirit of Truth will exit the world with the saints and there will be no further presence of God in the earth. The Devil will be allowed full reign during this time. It will be unimaginably dire to be left on the earth. To be left behind is to be eternally separated from God.

*The spiritual **"Clarion Call" is being sounded in the earth!!! Jesus is coming soon for the saints.** He loves mankind and He is warning of His imminent return. Take heed!*

O-O-O-O-O-O-O

5.5   The Power of the Cross

There is power in the name of Jesus. The power over some of the varied cases that came before Jesus is highlighted in this chapter.

The cross is depicted by suffering and shame yet the power of salvation and healing emanating from this selfless act is truly amazing. It is through the suffering and the shame that we can come to life in Christ Jesus. Everyone can have access to salvation because of the death, burial, and resurrection of our Lord Jesus. *(18) "But God shows his anger from heaven against all sinful, wicked people who suppress the truth by their wickedness. (19) They know the truth about God because he has made it obvious to them. (20) Forever since the world was created, people have seen the earth and sky. Through everything God made, they can clearly see his invisible qualities, his eternal power and divine nature. So they have no excuse for not knowing God" (Romans 1:18-20, NLT).* The preceding verses speak of the grace given to men that we have no excuse not to accept Jesus as Lord. We cannot refute the scriptural claims to His Lordship in the earth and His imminent return for those who will declare Him as Lord through their lives.

The spiritual climate is sapping the strength of the people. The demonic pressures have taken hold in a way that we have not seen before. We are being drawn into the state of "helplessness" because many have given up the fight to hold on and be strong. It is increasingly impossible for humankind to take control of their lives in a fashion they have known. The great ancient building blocks of the foundations of nations and communities have eroded and the dark waters of evil have compromised their strength. It is the power of the cross that will give mankind the solution to spiritually surface from all of life's challenges.

A holistic approach to healing is required to bring about a state of calm and fusion of our fragmented self. It comes through the prophetic Word foretold in Scripture of those times of refreshing. Through salvation, our spirits are watered and quenched from the thirst of sin. God has an appointed time with mankind to display His power and His glory that men will know that He is God, and the powers of darkness cannot continue to reign unabated. We are in that season of His power. The Scripture speaks of Jesus *"...whom heaven must receive until the time for restoring all the things about which God spoke by the mouth of his holy prophets long ago" (Acts 3:21, ESV)*.

5.6   The Unclean Spirit

The Scriptures refer to the "unclean spirit," *"Also a multitude gathered from the surrounding cities to Jerusalem, bringing sick people and those who were tormented by unclean spirits, and they were all healed (Acts 5:16).* It is a spiritually impure spirit. This spirit is behind the problems and the conditions nations and people are encountering. Jesus knew the spirit and sought only to rebuke and cast it out of the people he healed. The "arch" spirit of Satan indicates he is the chief architect behind the world systems and governments since the beginning of time. The impure spirit manipulates and controls soul territories and all entities of life. Once this territorial spirit gets a hold over these entities it is not easily broken. The unclean spirit is Beelzebub, "the prince of demons" (Luke 11:15). This universal spirit is responsible for the torments and destruction of communities and lives across this globe. The people hooked on drugs, drinks and all kinds of vices are victims of sin. These areas of human weaknesses are essentially a spiritual problem in the people. Many die in their condition not able to be liberated from the snares of the evil fowler.

5.7   'Who Touched Me?'

The story of the woman who made her way to Jesus with the flow of blood provides a heart-rending account of faith. According to Mark, this woman had done all that was humanly possible to be made well. Bereft of human solutions to her needs, she would have contemplated how to reach Jesus. She was sanctioned as "ceremonially unclean" and therefore, would be breaking the law to go through the crowd. Covertly, she made her way through the throng no doubt going to great lengths to conceal her identity. Her fear of recognition would have been palpable, but I believe this case was identified from the foundation of the world for the glory of God. Divine grace was upon her. She was in that condition for twelve years. God's perfect order of divine power and authority would be displayed as Jesus saw her making her way long before time began. It would be recorded in Scripture as a testament of God's power over the impure demonic realm.

Tentatively, she drew near to the Master hoping only to touch the hem of His garment and slip away unnoticed. The hem of His robe is thought to be the tassels that hung from His garment. Fixing her eyes on the tassels, she no doubt believed in her heart that by faith, just touching them would make her whole. When no one else can help to remedy the complaint, Jesus can. God looked down from heaven, and His compassion singled out this woman for release from the bond of affliction. Mercy saw her in her lonely desperate state. When no one cares and all hope fades, you can reach out and touch Jesus who is Lord over the curse of sin that blights the body, mind, spirit, and soul.

Jesus' question, *"Who touched me?"* may have alarmed her as she sought to remain anonymous. Tentatively, she declares, *"It was I who touched you."* Knowing how petrified she was, He reassured her with these endearing words. *"Daughter, your faith has healed you. Go in peace" (Luke 8:48, NIV).* The power of the tormentor was broken from that very moment.

5.8 'Be Thou Made Whole'

The ministry of Jesus was entire in that the people experienced salvation, healing, and deliverance from the tormentor behind their situation. They would also have experienced a better chance in life. The opportunity to work or to become socially included in their community would be open to them. The word of authority is released to bring healing and deliverance. "...*And He cast out the spirits with a word" (Matthew 8:16).* Every spirit that would militate against the Word to prevent healing and restoration was demolished at the cross. The will of God will be done to establish the kingdom of righteousness in the hearts of men.

The curse of sin is intended to waste the potential of lives and to destroy the individual. The impotent man spent a lifetime feeble and inadequate. Strong's Greek translation '*akrates*' means to be weak, powerless. '*kratos*' *(Strong's 2904)* is dominion, strength, power, a mighty deed. The word '*kratos*' depicts the qualities of our Lord Jesus who has dominion over the evil of unclean spirits afflicting the mind, body, spirit and soul of mankind.

The brief encounter of Jesus with the man crippled for thirty-eight years would change his life forever. He implored Jesus that He had no one to help him get into the troubled pool. No longer will there be a need to depend on others. There would be no need for his usual preamble of speech about his disability precluding him from getting into the water. It would be the last time he cried for help in his condition. The help of man is vain but Jesus has the authority and power to give and extend life. A Word spoken into the thirty-eight years' chronic situation caused the crippled man to gain strength to take steps of faith. He walked away healed from the place of his confinement. Jesus had ultimate power over the spirit behind the problem. The crippled man was no longer bound but reprieved from his chronic debilitating state as the chains of darkness were broken and torn away.

His strength to prevail as the Lion of Judah shall break every chain of evil bondage. All power has been given unto Jesus our

Lord in heaven and in the earth. He performed a mighty deed in the life of this impotent man.

5.9 'She Is Not Dead'

Jesus comes upon the scene of a community of mourners weeping for a little girl, twelve years who had just died. *"Now all wept and mourned for her; but He said, 'Do not weep; she is not dead, but sleeping.' And they ridiculed Him, knowing that she was dead. But He put them all outside, took her by the hand and called, saying, 'Little girl, arise.' Then her spirit returned, and she arose immediately. And He commanded that she be given something to eat" (Luke 8:41-55).*

When Jesus heard the news, He told the people not to weep because she was not dead. They laughed Him to scorn because the natural situation was indeed hopeless. The people viewed the situation through their natural eyes. Faith lets one see the situation from God's Word. Jesus said, "She is not dead." Jesus is the giver of life and a word from Him is accomplished regardless of how men see the situation. Standing on what God tells you in your situation is the key to procuring healing of all entities of your life. People will cause you to doubt your faith if you do not keep your spiritual eyes open to believe when the situation seems impossible.

5.10 Mary Magdalene

The women who surrounded Jesus' ministry came to Him knowing that their needs could only be met in Him. They loved Jesus. It was a pure love. Some writers portray Mary Magdalene as having been a worthless woman but there is no evidence in Scripture to suggest this. She was healed from an evil possession. In Him, the women found love and acceptance, contrary to the culture of bible times. Mary Magdalene was one such woman. She was a witness of the power of love to destroy the seven-fold strength of evil that gripped her life. How she came to be in that state is not known but what is known is that she was delivered from her bondage.

After a long and anxious night, it was Mary who quickly made her way to the tomb knowing Jesus was buried there. Even though Jesus told them of His resurrection she would have been surprised to realise that the body of her Saviour was no longer in the tomb. *"The first day of the week cometh Mary Magdalene early, when it was yet dark, unto the sepulchre, and seeth the stone taken away from the sepulchre" (John 20:1, KJV).* She would have gone in search of Him or to quickly spread the news. She was the first to see the risen Christ that resurrection morning. *"Now when he rose early on the first day of the week, he appeared first to Mary Magdalene, from whom he had cast out seven demons" (Mark 16:9, ESV).*

5.11 'Just Speak A Word'

"Wherefore neither thought I myself worthy to come unto thee: but say in a word, and my servant shall be healed" (Luke 7:7). Here is a case of a centurion, a man of authority under the Roman army, in charge of groups of centuries of around 100 soldiers. His servant was sick and he sought help from Jesus. Jesus was amazed at his great faith, of a kind He had not seen in all of Israel. The centurion did not want to trouble Jesus to come to his house. Rather, his faith made him ask that Jesus just speak a word and his servant would be healed. A word from God is enough to change a situation.

5.12 Deaf and Dumb Spirit

When Jesus called the twelve disciples to send forth, He gave them authority over the unclean spirits to cast them out and to heal all manner of diseases and all manner of sicknesses. He gave them instructions on how to conduct themselves. Jesus knew what they would encounter in the ministry of deliverance and healing. It is a ministry that Satan actively interferes with in order to obstruct the work of salvation to the lost.

Satan does not respect anyone. He seeks to destroy young and old, rich, poor, noble and ignoble, educated or unlearnt, it matters not. All nationalities and races of people are subject to the same foul spirits that destroy lives.

The deaf and dumb spirit is termed an 'unclean' spirit. *"And when Jesus saw that a crowd came running together, he rebuked the unclean spirit, saying to it, 'You mute and deaf spirit, I command you, come out of him and never enter him again'"* (Mark 9:25, ESV). This distressing case was of a young boy who suffered from an attack of this impure spirit. It caused him to convulse, scream and become rigid as though dead. The disciples were unable to cast out the demon from the young boy, but Jesus came upon the scene with a commanding higher level of authority and forbid the demons to enter another human soul.

The account in Matthew 9 shows the Pharisees, yet again, true to their character disrespecting the works of the Lord Jesus. As Jesus moved, a man who was demon -possessed and could not speak was brought to Jesus. After rebuking the demon, the man spoke and amazement caused the people to exclaim *"...Never was anything like this seen in Israel"* (Matthew 9:33, ESV). The only response befitting evil minds was to insult the Holy Spirit. They blasphemed and committed the eternal and unpardonable sin. *"...by the prince of the demons casteth he out demons"* (Matthew 9:34, ASV). Jesus therefore on healing the man with the deaf and dumb spirit took the opportunity to warn His disciples that if the Pharisees have called the master of the house Beelzebub how much more those who are of his household. We likewise will suffer for the gospel when we seek to stand against those who oppose the faith.

5.13 'Have Mercy On Me'

"And they came to Jericho. And as he was leaving Jericho with his disciples and a great crowd, Bartimaeus, a blind beggar, the son of Timaeus, was sitting by the roadside. And when he heard that it was Jesus of Nazareth, he began to cry out and say, 'Jesus, Son of David, have mercy on me!' And many rebuked him, telling

him to be silent. But he cried out all the more, 'Son of David, have mercy on me!'" (Mark 10:46-48, ESV).

Bartimaeus was blind and lived by begging from the people. It is likely they did not respect him. He was just the kind of person Jesus sought out amongst the people who followed Him. Jesus' ears and eyes were sharp to discern the needy and helpless. When he knew it was Jesus, he cried out, but the people wanted to gag him into being quiet. But faith would have it that he cried out all the more earnestly. This was his opportunity to be healed, and he determined in his spirit to be heard by Jesus. Jesus seized the chance to call him forward. *(51)"And Jesus said to him, 'What do you want me to do for you?' And the blind man said to him, 'Rabbi, let me recover my sight.' (52) And Jesus said to him, 'Go your way; your faith has made you well.' And immediately he recovered his sight and followed him on the way" (Mark 10:51-52, ESV).*

5.14   A Raging Fever

"And when Jesus entered Peter's house, he saw his mother-in-law lying sick with a fever. He touched her hand, and the fever left her, and she rose and began to serve him" (Matthew 8:14-15, ESV). Jesus who bore our sickness and carried our sorrows is acquainted with our suffering. He had a compassionate heart and became the servant of the people. In this case, Peter's mother-in-law was able to immediately resume her domestic chores. She began to serve Jesus and the disciples. The power behind the fever was completely and immediately destroyed.

5.15   Spirit of Infirmity

This woman was a Jewish woman as mention is made of her as the daughter of Abraham. She was afflicted by Satan who kept her bound all those years. It did not go unnoticed by the religious cohorts who objected to her healing on the Sabbath day. *"And, behold, there was a woman which had a spirit of infirmity eighteen years, and was bowed together, and could in no wise lift up herself. And when Jesus saw her, he called her to him, and said unto her, Woman, thou art loosed from thine infirmity. And he laid his hands on her: and immediately she was made straight, and glorified God" (Luke 13:11-13, KJV).* She was bowed over with a curvature of her spine for eighteen years. When Jesus met her, He commanded that she be loosed and the spirit of infirmity left her. She was made whole immediately. She rejoiced praising God for her deliverance.

5.16   Place of Mercy

Bethesda means "house of mercy." How ironic that the place of mercy was where many could not receive their deliverance. The servant of mercy would give credence to the meaning of the "house of mercy." Jesus passing by brought hope to the people who had lain along the sideways languishing in their pitiable state. The impotent man was one who joyfully received his deliverance. The radiant glory of Jesus' presence filled the atmosphere with expectation, hope, joy, and excitement because the impossibilities confronting the people would now give way to possibilities. Healing could now be for everyone and not for just for the "privileged" minority who could help themselves physically or by other means.

The transforming light explodes in the heart of the believer because of the magnetism of Jesus' glory. The spiritual veil of darkness is ripped away from the heart and the floodlight of His brilliance fills the atmosphere.

The five colonnades where these people gathered have significance when you consider that the number five is "grace." Oh, what measure of grace for the impotent souls! As Jesus passed by He brought healing and deliverance to the sick and dying lying by the wayside. Grace has been afforded mankind through the Passover Lamb. John the Baptist, His forerunner, on seeing Jesus announced to the people *"Behold, the Lamb of God, who takes away the sin of the world!"(John 1:29, ESV).* Through the memorial name of our Lord, we can have passage from spiritual death to life.

"For there is a fountain filled with blood drawn from Immanuel's vein and sinners plunge beneath the flood and lose all their guilty stains." "E'er since by faith I saw the stream, thy flowing wounds supply, redeeming grace has been my theme and shall be till I die." This hymnal written by *William Cowper (1772)* is poignantly versed. This was a man diagnosed with madness in *(1763),* yet, nine years later he wrote the song above. How sickness can isolate one unable to communicate his feelings he was socially condemned. Trapped in himself he drew solace from his intimacy with God. No one could draw him out of the obscurity he found himself in. However, his faith in God was telling. To write such a universally appealing hymn would serve to bring some measure of healing to his pain. He would have written out of his inner experience of gloominess. We are all wretched and miserable souls without the grace of our Lord Jesus.

5.17 'Take Up Your Mat'

"Jesus said to him, Get up, take up thy bed, and walk" (John 5:8, ESV). Here is a case of a crippled man lying on a crude mobile construction and Jesus comes along and takes authority over the situation. The man was immediately healed on this Sabbath day. He walked away but was confronted by a group of Jewish leaders who told him he had broken the law. His sin was carrying his mat on the Sabbath. He protested that the man who healed him told him to take up his mat and walk. They demanded he tell them who the person was. This exchange was not about the mat, it was about the healing of the people on the Sabbath. Satan is behind the angst of these leaders because his plan is to avert the work of Christ's kingdom. This cohort, objectionable to Jesus' ministry knew it was the Christ who had done such a marvellous deliverance. Yet again, we see the anti-Christ spirit at work trying to thwart the work of salvation.

5.18 'I Say to You Rise'

"As he drew near to the gate of the town, behold, a man who had died was being carried out, the only son of his mother, and she was a widow, and a considerable crowd from the town was with her" (Luke 7:12, ESV). Jesus had gone with his disciples to a place called Nain meaning "beautiful." This village is situated outside Jerusalem, in proximity to Mount Tabor. The people of the village had gathered around to support this mother and when Jesus saw the funeral procession, He was moved with compassion. He drew near and touched the bier and said: "Young man, I say to you rise."

PART SIX

AUTHORITY IN THE WORD

"Behold, I have given you authority to tread upon serpents and scorpions, and over all the power of the enemy: and nothing shall in any wise hurt you"

(Luke 10:19,ASV**)**

6.1   Pots of Clay

We are encouraged that we have the rich treasure of kingdom authority embedded deep in the foundations of our being. It is heavenly resources at our disposal. We can draw from the source when the situation demands heavenly assistance. Jesus is the capstone in our foundations releasing the power given to us. As vessels, we are formed from the dust of the earth. It is in these pots of clay that heavenly power has been deposited through Jesus Christ. *"But we have this treasure in earthen vessels, that the excellence of the power may be of God and not of us. We are hard-pressed on every side, yet not crushed; we are perplexed, but not in despair; persecuted, but not forsaken; struck down, but not destroyed–always carrying about in the body the dying of the Lord Jesus, that the life of Jesus also may be manifested in our body"* (2 Corinthians 4:7-10, KJV).

The Scriptures illustrate that the power is not of ourselves lest we should boast as carriers of the divine anointing. We are mere vessels suitably endowed with grace and robust in the faith to be used by God. Jesus is the giver and He admonished the disciples to keep their enthusiasm in perspective. When we have preached to others, raised the dead, and healed the sick, let us not be destroyed by the enemy and miss out on eternal life. *"Nevertheless, do not rejoice in this, that the spirits are subject to you, but rejoice that your names are written in heaven"* (Luke 10:20, ESV).

There is a discipline that marks one out for kingdom authority. To exercise the power given unto us through Jesus Christ, it requires the study of the Word and a prayerful disposition coupled with fasting as necessitated by the Spirit. We must not become religious through continual fasting but be directed by the Spirit. Wisdom is urged, as it is the plan of the enemy to cause one to cross over the fine line of being spirit-led and being drawn subtly into religious activities.

The Lord's commendation and assessment of our works are never by the measure or quantified by the amount. It is determined by the quality of service. The state of the heart is the means by which we are validated and rewarded. It is God who has the power to promote and demote according to His standard of justice. Holiness through His Word is a prerequisite to acceptance by God. Then, with a thankful and obedient heart, He will entrust us with the keys to kingdom authority. *(1) "And he called the twelve together, and gave them power and authority over all demons, and to cure diseases. (2) And He sent them forth to preach the kingdom of God, and to heal the sick " (Luke 9:1,* ASV*)*.

We must be grateful to Jesus the giver. It is He who has set us free from past sins and as broken pottery He has recast us into His likeness. His reign in us validates us in the service of God. Obedience is an integral quality for lawful kinship with Christ. Also, His justice and righteousness are continually working for us in this body of clay. They are eternal tenets in the foundation of our faith. Therefore, we are justified by faith and made righteous through salvation and these two inextricably linked virtues are the epitome of our Lord Jesus.

6.2   Censorship

My crude translation of censorship is an officially orchestrated control over groups or materials in order to curtail civil liberty. It is not intended to imply a negative exercise but what I can deduce from censorship is that it is a form of control to regulate an area of human life.

After 70 years of exile in Babylon, in the fullness of time, God roused Cyrus, king of Persia to proclaim the rebuilding of the temple in Jerusalem. It was time for the people of God to be back on their own soil with a national identity. We see from the biblical accounts in Ezra and Nehemiah that the devastation of Jerusalem was great. It covered all areas of national life. It was, therefore, necessary to galvanise the efforts of the returning Jews to re-establish and affirm their true heritage.

Areas of civil life would be censored and curtailed to ensure that the nation returned to their rightful legacy of their forefathers. The Jewish customs, values, and beliefs were long eroded from the minds of the people as they descended into spiritual, moral and cultural deprivation in a strange land. It was time to identify the true Israelites and instill what is their legitimate birthright. Even matters pertaining to the sacred order of the temple had been violated under captivity.

For instance, it was the custom in bible times that matters pertaining to the temple must be overseen by a true Israeli. Through the public records, it would come to light that foreign labourers were forbidden to go into the temple. There was a class of true Israelites appointed to service in the office as temple servants. Therefore, censorship would ensure that only those of pure Jewish heritage by parental lineage would help in the temple rebuilding and also the overall reconstruction of the city. The legitimacy of the heads of the household of the families was ascertained by searching through the public records.

The reconstruction programme necessitated the reinstating of the sacred laws in the order of all aspects of Jewish life. The emergence of the diaspora of the Jewish people from captivity meant that many had waned in their commitment to God. It was imperative that as an emerging nation they reaffirm their allegiance to the laws of God. It was imperative that the law was embedded in the national mind once again. The memories of captivity that brought many into idolatry and spiritual bondage would be stripped away by the recommitting of adherence to the laws of God.

The business of consolidating the religious entity of the rebuilding of the nation was conducted under the auspices of Ezra the prophet. The Scriptures say that he had set his heart to seek the laws of Jehovah and to do them, and also to teach in Israel the statutes and ordinances of God (Ezra 7: 10).

6.3 'Who Is Your Daddy?'

Nehemiah was one of the spiritual leaders faced with overseeing the reconstruction of the destroyed city of Jerusalem. Aggrieved in his spirit, he was led by the Spirit to survey the damage done to the walls of the city. He sought to consult the public register to ascertain how the land was originally divided and the genealogy of the people. The task at hand would require the heads of families and the workers to be authentic Jews recorded in the public ancestry register. As mentioned earlier, the stipulation was that they could not be foreigners and proof that they were descendants of Israel was required. They were listed as appointees to serve and the censorship of Israeli identity was undertaken by their genealogy.

The Assyrians were neighbours but the hostility between them and God's people was longstanding. These pagan adversaries of Judah and Benjamin would not make the work at hand easy but sought ways to circumvent their effort. When they saw that the diaspora was intending to rebuild after years of destruction they conspired by offering to help. They approached Zerubbabel and the heads of the families with their proposal only to be rebuffed. *"But Zerubbabel, Jeshua, and the rest of the heads of fathers' houses in Israel said to them, "You have nothing to do with us in building a house to our God; but we alone will build to the LORD, the God of Israel as King Cyrus the king of Persia has commanded us"* (Ezra 4:3). The Assyrians, angered by the rejection, schemed to hinder them with further confrontations and opposition to the rebuilding programme.

As Christians, our heavenly Father is God. We come under the blood of Jesus Christ. Our heritage is in Him and our identity is legitimised by the qualities of the kingdom of God. What qualifies us to use the authority of the Word is our identity in God. We are searched by the Spirit of God to ensure our true identity. The enemy knows when our identity is in Jesus and he will seek to restrain our work in the kingdom. Jesus said to the seventy disciples He sent forth that they should not rejoice because the evil spirits were subject to them, but that their names are written in the Book of Life. That is the official record of our true identity. It is not by works lest we should boast but that we are judged worthy to be counted amongst those of the household of God. Belonging to the spiritual lineage through the blood of Jesus Christ. *"Now therefore ye are no more strangers and foreigners, but fellow citizens with the saints, and of the household of God; and are built upon the foundation of the apostles and prophets, Jesus Christ himself being the chief corner stone"(Ephesians 2:20, KJV).*

6.4 'Who Are You?'

Using the Word in the name of Jesus is the believers' authority. His name is great to demolish the works of evil. It is a territorial name of power that offers protection against any hostile powers. The name of Jesus commands respect in the demonic realm to influence and control powers. The Devil knows those without authority who are using the name of Jesus without any spiritual weight. To command spirits to evict their place of residency is to engage in territorial warfare. Demons are resident spirits reluctant to evacuate a place they call home. They will put up a fight. It is a foolish and futile venture to engage with demons without spiritual authority in the name of Jesus.

Sceva was one of the high priests based in Jerusalem and he had seven sons. The sons were part of a known peripatetic group of prophets. These foolish young men attempted to command evil spirits to come out of a young man who was demon possessed. *"A group of Jews was traveling from town to town casting out evil spirits. They tried to use the name of the Lord Jesus in their incantation, saying, "I command you in the name of Jesus, whom Paul preaches, to come out!" (Acts 19:13, NLT).* Their audacity to seek to cast out the spirits by feigning the power that Paul, the apostle possessed in the name of Jesus was to evoke a serious backlash from the demons. *"But the evil spirit answered them, 'Jesus I know, and Paul I recognise, but who are you?'" (Acts 19:15, ESV).* It was an unwise decision by these men to adjure the spirits to come out without any spiritual right to control the situation. Immediately the spirits savagely set upon them. They were beaten and humiliated by the violent man who was under a perfect work of control by the legions of spirits.

6.5   Spirit of Truth

When Jesus left the earth, He told His disciples that the Comforter would come *"But the Advocate, the Holy Spirit, whom the Father will send in my name, will teach you all things and will remind you of everything I have said to you" (John 14:26),* and He would reside permanently with them representing God in man. *(16) "And I will ask the Father, and he will give you another Helper, to be with you forever, (17) even the Spirit of truth, whom the world cannot receive, because it neither sees him nor knows him. You know him, for he dwells with you and will be in you" (John 14:16-17, ESV).*

The Comforter is the Spirit of truth that has come to convict men of their sins. His truth is the Word of God. There is no private interpretation of the Scriptures, and it is the Spirit of truth that will ensure that we all articulate coherently with one voice to the world concerning who Jesus is. *"When the Spirit of truth shall come He will guide you in all things" (John 16:13, NLT).*

For there will be many in the last days who will come with convincing words purporting their works in the name of Jesus. *"The Spirit clearly says that in later times some will abandon the faith and follow deceiving spirits and things taught by demons" (1Timothy 4:1, NIV).* Their true intent is to draw people away from the message of hope and healing. According to Jude, they are devils denying our Lord. They follow their natural instincts and have not the Spirit of God. They are not abiding in the Word and so follow the course of their evil hearts. *"For certain people have crept in unnoticed who long ago were designated for this condemnation, ungodly people, who pervert the grace of our God into sensuality and deny our only Master and Lord, Jesus Christ"(Jude 1:4).* They show respect of persons only for the sake of their own advantage. They have not the Spirit of truth abiding in them.

It is a fearful accord by Jude. It is the role of the Holy Spirit to keep God's people in the truth of the Word. He will present us faultless before the Father who loves us and desire above all things that we prosper in the health of the Word.

6.6   Jesus our Example

Jesus was a prophet sent to teach us in the true and living way. His righteousness is the effectual hallmark of our faith to attest to our character and authenticity in Him.

Jesus, therefore, led His disciples by example, and He always sought to be with His father in prayer. Drawn away from the crowd to a place of solitude, He was refreshed in His spirit as the people drew from Him spiritual strength.

Jesus always enquired or remarked on the faith of the seeker. One must be a willing participant of his/her healing. "Wilt thou be made whole?" "What do you want me to do for you?" These are pertinent questions because faith is the conduit to tap into the source of His power.

In looking at how Jesus exercised His authority, He nearly always followed a 4-fold pattern. I believe this is the model used by Jesus to cast out demons:

(1) Firstly, Jesus will rebuke a demon. Sometimes He instructs them to be silent,

(2) Secondly, He commands the evil spirit to come out of the oppressed person.

(3) Thirdly, Jesus commands the Spirit of healing to be restored to the individual.

(4) Jesus usually gives an instruction to the individual.

("Go and sin no more" *John 8:11)*

("Go home to your family and tell them what the Lord has done for you" *Mark 5:19).*

("Go, wash in the pool of Siloam" *John 9:7).*

("Give her something to eat", *Mark 5:43).*

He also told the lepers to go and inform the authorities and offer the sacrifice required of them according to the law. Jesus was not a lawbreaker, but He would not allow the law to prevent Him from doing God's work for the people.

6.7   Keys To Unlock The Curse

All power belongs to the Son of God, and He knows those who are His. "…"*And Jesus came and spake unto them, saying. All power is given unto me in heaven and in earth" (Matthew 28:18, ESV).* The power over all kingdoms, realms, and nations is ultimately under the authority and control of Jesus as confirmed by His Word. *(18)" And I tell you, you are Peter, and on this rock I will build my church, and the gates of hell shall not prevail against it. (19) I will give you the keys of the kingdom of heaven, and whatever you bind on earth shall be bound in heaven, and whatever you loose on earth shall be loosed in heaven." (Matthew 16:18-19, ESV)* Here the scriptures give understanding to Jesus being the Rock of His kingdom of righteousness. There is no power that can stand against it. The keys are symbolic of authority and access. To those whom He has entrusted His power, they have right to exercise the authority in His name.

6.8   Keys of Authority

The revelation of who Jesus is and His power over the works of darkness are revealed through the Spirit. *"All things have been committed to me by my Father. No one knows the Son except the Father, and no one knows the Father except the Son and those to whom the Son chooses to reveal him (Matthew 11:27, ESV).* The keys bring with them responsibility and spiritual weight. They are entrusted to those who are called by Jesus' name.

In Isaiah 22 an oracle was given concerning the Valley of Vision. This place is thought to be where God revealed himself in visions. Possibly one of the gorges situated just outside the city of Jerusalem. The context to this chapter is one of sorrow for Isaiah the prophet because the people of Jerusalem were steeped in self-indulgence and oblivious to their spiritual state. They left off seeking the guidance of God as instructed by Isaiah and looked to other means of self-help.

Isaiah is sent to give a word to Shebna who was a foreigner in charge of the palace. He was not the rightful leader that God chose. As a foreigner he had no legitimate right to his position. But the inherent nature of God's people caused them to intermingle at all levels. In the fullness of time Shebna would be thrust out and his carnal motives revealed. *(15) "This is what the Lord, the LORD Almighty, says: "Go, say to this steward, to Shebna the palace administrator: (16) What are you doing here and who gave you permission to cut out a grave for yourself here, hewing your grave on the height and chiseling your resting place in the rock? (17) "Beware, the LORD is about to take firm hold of you and hurl you away, you mighty man. (Isaiah 22:15-17, NIV)* God would remove him from office and give his position to Eliakim, a steward who was considered more deserving although he was weak in his position. It was Eliakim who would be given the keys to the Royal House. The keys to the House of David would be placed upon his shoulders. He would have the authority to shut and open the doors of the Royal House and no one could come against him.

The Eternal Father of the universe bestowed honour, eternal authority, and sovereign power upon Jesus as King, His Beloved One. He will also give this power to those He has called or chosen for service. Jesus said, *"And these signs will accompany those who believe: in my name they will cast out demons; they will speak in new tongues" (Mark 16:17, ESV).* He will give the keys of authority to break curses to those who will permit Him to reign in their hearts. His kingdom is without end, and He came to set up His kingdom of righteousness here on earth. All the people of the earth who will accept Jesus as Lord will have Him seated at the helm of their lives. It is only then that mankind is in a position to exercise with power the weaponry of the Word of God. We have the spiritual legal right to exercise our authority in the name of Jesus and to break every curse from the spiritual fall of mankind. We can demonstrate the resurrection power by taking down and demolishing the kingdom of darkness in the hearts of men with the healing Word.

The healing, restoration and reconciliation to the Father can only take place in the name of our Lord Jesus. We have no other authority to spiritual healing and restoration in the course of human life and entities except by using the authority as given to us in the Word. *"Then he called his twelve disciples together, and gave them power and authority over all devils, and to cure diseases" (Luke 9:1 ESV).*

We are in a season where the world is talking about healing and restoration. These concepts have not come about by man, but the Spirit of God has ushered in the season for the manifestation of the power of God. There are many means whereby people can have healing in body and mind but inner healing of the spirit man comes through salvation. People who are not using the power of the Word when they talk about spiritual healing and forgiveness are advocating a service not authenticated by God. It is only God who can forgive sins. *(2) "Praise Yahweh, my soul, and don't forget all his benefits (3) who forgives all your sins, who heals all your diseases; (4) who redeems your life from destruction..." (Psalms 102:2-5, WEB).* There is no power to bring about forgiveness, divine healing or spiritual restoration except through Jesus who is the minister of reconciliation.

6.9   Authority In The Name of Jesus

The government of Jesus' kingdom is the key that has been placed upon our shoulders. *"For to us a child is born, to us a son is given; and the government shall be upon his shoulder, and his name shall be called Wonderful Counselor, Mighty God, Everlasting Father, Prince of Peace." (Isaiah 9:6, ESV)* Like

Eliakim, Jesus has placed spiritual influence and power upon our shoulders. This power and right have been graciously conferred upon those who will believe on the Lord Jesus and do His will. We did not deserve such an honour but Mercy spoke for us. Eliakim was found worthy but he was ineffective in his office. God will robe his servant in His righteousness and give them spiritual power over the realm of darkness to be effective and strong against the contending forces against the kingdom of God.

One must confess Jesus as Lord and repent of their sins committed. The possibilities are endless for those who will strive to walk in the knowledge of God's Word. The power of the Word knows no bounds to release the people from stagnation and limitations. *"And Jesus came and spake unto them, saying, all power is given unto me in heaven and in earth" (Matthew 28:18, KJV)*. Again, Jesus said, *"Behold, I have given you authority to tread on serpents and scorpions, and over all the power of the enemy, and nothing shall hurt you" (Luke 10:19, ESV)*. We can do all things through the strength of our Lord.

What God has placed in earthen vessels is absolutely astounding. We cannot comprehend the power from on high that has been bestowed upon mere mortals through the authoritative name of Jesus our Lord. Jesus in us is greater than the spirit and powers of this world. Understanding the authority we have in the name of Jesus commands the submission of the lesser power, Satan. His works over the lives of the people are subdued and demolished in the name of Jesus. The Scriptures say, *"That at the name of Jesus every knee should bow, in heaven and on earth and under the earth" (Philippians 2:10, Berean Study Bible)*. Further, every tongue shall acknowledge God *"...for it is written, 'As I live, says the Lord, every knee shall bow to me, and every tongue shall confess to God'" (Romans 14:11, ESV)*. Even demons admit that Jesus is Lord. *"And demons also came out of many, crying, 'You are the Son of God!' But he rebuked them and would not allow them to speak, because they knew that he was the Christ" (Luke 4:41, ESV)*. We have the power in the authority of the Word to bind the dark forces of evil and loose the Spirit of healing in Jesus name.

The powers of the darkness of this age have blinded the spiritual eyes of the people and they are unable to discern the times we are now living in. Yet, as Jesus said they can discern the sky to determine the weather if it will be a fair or foul day. Spiritual deprivation holds men in torment and fear. The Devil has put barriers in place to hinder and block the flow of the work of the Spirit to bring repentance and healing. There is no will in the hearts of the people to consciously take heed to God's Word concerning the work of grace even when the end time is imminent. *"Satan, who is the god of this world, has blinded the minds of those who don't believe. They are unable to see the glorious light of the Good News. They don't understand this message about the glory of Christ, who is the exact likeness of God"* (2 Corinthians 4 v 4, NLT).

6.10   Called to the Kingdom

The people of God are called to the kingdom of righteousness to carry on the work of our Lord. It is for such a time as this that we must make our calling and election sure. We are expected to extend His ministry of reconciliation to a dying world. The power of healing that He began in our being is for the entire human race. Jesus gave those keys to His followers so that they could unlock and access, by the power of His Spirit those regions holding men captive. This is all made possible by having the authority in His name to disable the activity of evil. All those who will declare Jesus as Lord are the recipients of the same promises He gave to the disciples. *"But ye shall receive power, when the Holy Spirit is come upon you: and ye shall be my witnesses both in Jerusalem, and in all Judea and Samaria, and unto the utmost part of the earth"* (Acts 1:8, ASV). Without any reservation, we can boldly declare Jesus as Lord over the demonic realm and nothing can by any means harm us. Jesus is the Word of authority and He will not let us down when we exercise this power in His name.

6.11   Getting our Priorities Right

"And the seventy returned again with joy, saying, Lord, even the

devils are subject unto us through thy name" (Luke 10:17, ESV). There is no joy in having demons subjected to us through the name of Jesus. When we have commanded the spirits to leave, we should humbly ask God to keep us from any backlash of the enemy. The joy in doing God's work is that our names are recorded in the Book of Life. For many shall come saying "Lord did we not cast out devils in your name?" But Jesus said to them, "Depart from me I know thee not." Why would Jesus dismiss those who cast out demons supposedly in His name? Our service to God is judged by the quality of our hearts and not by the works lest we should boast. If we do our works with an imperfect heart, God will overlook your efforts and seek out those whose hearts are true. It is the desire of the Lord that we cast out demons in His name. However, to do it with impure intents and actions is to forfeit the blessings that come from true service to God.

6.12   The 7-Fold Strength of Evil

In Matthew 17, the case of a young boy bound by a demon is narrated. The young lad is often gripped by a seizure, when distressed he seeks to self-harm. It is a pitiable condition and the father sought help from Jesus. As he knelt before Him, he said; *"Lord, have mercy on my son, for he is an epileptic and he suffers terribly. For often he falls into the fire, and often into the water" (Matthew 17:14, ESV).* The father had previously sought help from the disciples. However, they could not heal the child. Yeshua answered and He said, *"Oh, faithless and twisted generation! How long shall I be with you, and how long shall I endure you? Bring him here to me" (Matthew 17:17, Aramaic Bible).* Jesus then rebuked the demon and the child was healed immediately.

The disciples then approached Jesus to enquire why they were unable to bring healing to the distressed young boy. Jesus' response was that they had so little faith and the kind of stronghold in the boy required a greater level of power. *"... A greater level of faith through fasting and prayer to cast out those demons that are so strong" (Mark 9:17-29. ESV). "Howbeit, these kinds goeth not out but by prayer and fasting." (Matthew 17:21, KJV).*

6.13   The Power of the Word

It is the Word of God that expels demons and heals the sick. Our efforts to use powerful language to destroy curses and obliterate evil are just expressions of our intent. It is the Scriptures that contain the power. *"And they were astonished at His teaching, for His word possessed authority" (Luke 4:32).* Every word from God has the power to demolish arguments, destroy evil constructions, and obliterate bonds of iniquity. When the Word is spoken it accomplishes what is intended because it cannot go back to God void of its legal force.

The satanic yokes over the people and all entities of their lives tie the potential for spiritual development. The released Word brought inspiring and new meaning to life. The people were sick and destitute, and they needed a Saviour. Hence, they thronged Jesus as He traversed around the cities and countryside doing the will of His father.

PART SEVEN
JESUS IS LORD

"I persevered in demonstrating among you the marks of a true apostle, including signs, wonders and miracles."

(2 Corinthians 12:12,NIV)

"And these signs shall follow them that believe; in my name shall they cast out devils..."

(Mark 16:17)

In this section, I will illustrate the power that God has placed in us.

7.1   Broken Pieces of Clay

Mankind is from the dust of the earth, hence, the reference to earthenware. As pots of clay, we have become cracked and broken. *"O Israel, can I not do to you as this potter has done to his clay? As the clay is in the potter's hand, so are you in my hand." (Jeremiah 18:6, NLT).* We are marred in the Master's hand. It is thought that David in Palms 51 alludes to his experience as a man broken by his human weaknesses. The prophet Nathan exposes his sin with Bathsheba. It was an episode that caused David much anguish of heart as he regrettably mulled over his shame and painful actions. What God loved about David is his contrite spirit to repent. We had been left on the refuse heap of life. Jesus has come along, and lovingly He has picked up the pieces of the lives of countless millions of people from all tribes and nations who have accepted His invitation to salvation.

Jesus' ministry of salvation and restoration has repaired the breached areas of human life. There is forgiveness and healing from violating God's law. The spiritual fissures of our lives are mended. The discarded pieces have been put together again. We can now hold the spiritual treasure that God has given to men in clay pots.

We have been made whole once again. We are now able to live peaceably with God and man. We can now become servants of righteousness empowered with the Spirit of God to do great and mighty works of faith in the name of Jesus.

7.2   Receiving the Lord Jesus

We can only do the work of God if we have accepted Jesus as Lord of our lives.

To receive Jesus into your heart is a simple step of faith. So uncomplicated and easy is the process of acceptance of faith that many are left wondering if they really are saved. Yes, you are! Your acceptance of faith is not validated by emotions or any other factors. It is simply to believe, to confess, and to accept Jesus as your Saviour.

Salvation was first to the Jews simply because Jesus came out of a Jewish lineage and then to the Gentiles who were intended recipients of the faith. *"For God so loved the world that He gave His only Begotten Son that whosoever shall believe on Him shall be saved" (John 3:16, ESV).* The Jews rejected Jesus and the Gentiles (anyone who is a non-Jew) being the wild olive tree that was engrafted into the true Branch that is recorded as being Jesus Christ Himself. The Branch represents the rich root of the olive tree, an analogy of the Jewish nation. The apostles were bearers of the Good News and stirred by the love, compassion, and the joy of their salvation—they turned their world upside down. With enthusiasm, they roused the listeners and defiantly propagated the Word across the hostile nations.

7.3   A 3-Fold Key to Salvation

Key 1:

Do you believe that Jesus is the Son of God?

"Whoever confesses that Jesus is the Son of God, God abides in him, and he in God" (1 John 4:15, ESV).

Key 2:

Do you believe that He died for your sins?

"Who gave Himself for our sins to deliver us from the present evil age, according to the will of our God and Father" (Galatians 1:4, ESV).

Key 3:

Do you believe that He is able to forgive you of your sins?

"Because, if you confess with your mouth that Jesus is

Lord, and believe in your heart that God raised Him from the dead, you will be saved" (Romans 10:9-11,ESV).

If you can willingly answer *YES* to those three questions and decide to follow Jesus, you are saved. Firstly, it is based on believing in Jesus as Lord and the Son of God who came and died on the cross to deliver men from their sins. Secondly, on confession that you are a sinner needing salvation, you intentionally open the door of your heart to invite the Lord Jesus into your life. The confession of your sins completes the process. It is a spiritual mystery that we cannot comprehend but from that moment you have the assistance of heaven on your side as you are accepted into the kingdom of God. Someone can then take you through a prayer. If you are doing this alone, you can personalise the prayer in Luke that Jesus taught His disciples. It is a simple but a succinct prayer, acknowledging the Father as provider and helper in our weaknesses. *(2) "And He said to them, when you pray, say: 'Father, hallowed be your name. Your kingdom come. (3) Give us each day our daily bread. (4) And forgive us our sins, For we ourselves also forgive everyone who is indebted to us. And lead us not into temptation" (Luke 11:1-4,ESV).*

Now that we are reconciled to God, we can become witnesses of the hope we have in Christ Jesus. *"For God wanted them to know that the riches and glory of Christ are for you Gentiles, too. And this is the secret: Christ lives in you. This gives you the assurance of sharing his glory" (Colossians 1:27,NLT).* Those who have come to know Jesus have embarked on an incredible spiritually rewarding journey. It is the most life-transforming and purpose fulfilling experience one can ever undertake. The journey has its challenges and tests but at those junctures, one is strengthened in the faith to endure the arduous efforts that spiritually pay dividends.

7.4   The Comforter

When Jesus left the earth after His resurrection, He told His disciples that He was going away but He would send the Comforter. The Comforter is the Holy Spirit. He was sent by Jesus to accompany His people in the world. *"But you will receive power when the Holy Spirit has come upon you, and you will be my witnesses in Jerusalem and in all Judea and Samaria, and to the end of the earth" (Acts 1:8, ESV).* There has always been a presence of the Godhead in the earth realm. At no time since the beginning of time has the world been absent of God's presence. Before Jesus came to earth, God was with man. Jesus came and dwelt with us and after His mission to bring salvation and healing, He left the earth. He sent the Spirit of Truth who now resides within the hearts of those who believe on the Lord Jesus. *"And I will ask the Father, and he will give you another Helper, to be with you forever" (John 14:16, ESV).*

The role of the Spirit is to empower and prepare the people of God for service. *"And they were all filled with the Holy Spirit and began to speak in other tongues as the Spirit gave them utterance" (Luke 2:4, ESV).* The Holy Spirit initiates and convicts men of their sins and brings about true repentance. He is the revealer of God's truth in the heart. The Spirit of God exposes the works of darkness. There is, therefore, nothing hidden that will not be exposed and made known by the seven eyes of God before His throne. *"The time is coming when everything that is covered up will be revealed, and all that is secret will be made known to all" (Luke 12:2, NLT).* I believe we are in that season of revelation when God will reveal the sins of the people on the housetops if they do not repent. The deeds that are covered will be made known publicly.

7.5   Dependency Upon the Giver

Paul the apostle, a remarkable man was afflicted in his body and as he sought his healing, the Lord reassured him that he was taken care of. Paul then accepted that in his suffering he was able to bear all things because the power of the cross was enough for him. Lest we should boast, we are constantly reminded that our adequacy in the mission entrusted to us is only made possible through our dependency on God. The Bible records he suffered from a "thorn" in his flesh. It is not clear from the Scriptures what his problem was, but the Lord comforted His beloved servant with the grace that he needed to overcome his suffering. In prayer, the Lord ministered these words to him three times. *"'My grace is all you need. My power works best in weakness.' So now I am glad to boast about my weaknesses, so that the power of Christ can work through me"* *(2 Corinthians 12:9, NLT).*

The Giver of the gift requires that we humbly submit ourselves to His leading. It is at the feet of Jesus that we are able to be a blessing. It is an honour to be chosen in the service of God. It is fitting that we fall down at the feet of our Lord and worship in gratitude. The vessels possessing the anointing that God has bestowed upon mere flesh must be clean and holy unto Him.

7.6   Greater Works We Will Do

"Truly, truly, I say to you, whoever believes in me will also do the works that I do; and greater works than these will he do, because I am going to the Father" *(John 14:12, ESV).* It is the empowerment of the Holy Spirit that prepares the servants of God to be endowed with the gift of healing. The disciples waited eagerly in the upper room for the Spirit of Truth, and their expectation in God was not disappointed. *"If you then, who are evil, know how to give good gifts to your children, how much more will the heavenly Father give the Holy Spirit to those who ask him!"* *(Luke 11:13, ESV).*

It is God who chooses the vessels He will use for the demonstration of His divine power. The apostles were witnesses of Jesus' ministry, and they were keen to move in the grace and favour anointing so that others could experience the signs, miracles and wonders of the ministry of reconciliation. The mystery of the Word dwelling in humankind has a transforming effect on our lives through His love, His humility, and His truth. The glorious hope of the Spirit breathing, enlivening, and rejuvenating our being is visibly experienced through spiritual works of righteousness. We are able to be as victorious as our Lord because He has given unto us this measure of blessing. *"Behold, I give unto you power to tread on serpents and scorpions, and over all the power of the enemy and nothing shall by any means hurt you" (Luke 10:19, KJV).*

7.7   Anointed and Empowered

The apostle Paul was one of the most spiritually effective and ardent witnesses of Jesus. His passion and boldness transformed communities and lives as he traversed the regions of the Gentiles after Jesus departed from the earth.

God was with Paul as he was with Jesus of Nazareth. He anointed Paul with the Holy Spirit and with power. He was emboldened with the anointing and ceased not to declare the power of the cross even when imprisoned and ostracised. Note that the Scriptures say that Jesus was baptised with the Holy Spirit and with power. *"...anointed Jesus of Nazareth with the Holy Spirit and with power. He went about doing good and healing all who were oppressed by the devil, for God was with him" (Acts 10:38, ESV).* A distinction is made with the baptism of the Holy Spirit and the power. Therefore, there is a level of power that we should seek to operate in for the ministry of healing and deliverance.

7.8   Unusual Power by God

Furthermore, it is God who sets forth His apostles because He is with them. What God gives to His servants is for the benefit of the people. All the glory belongs to God for only He can forgive people of their sins, heal the people and deliver the captives from the heavy chains that bind them. *"But we have this treasure in earthen vessels, that the excellency of the power may be of God, and not of us"* (2 Corinthians 4:7, KJV). We must submit ourselves to the authority of God for greater is He that is in us than he that is in the world (1 John 4:4).

The apostle Paul was one of those whom God did unusual works by his hands. *(11) "And God was doing extraordinary miracles by the hands of Paul, (12) so that even handkerchiefs or aprons that had touched his skin were carried away to the sick, and their diseases left them and the evil spirits came out of them" (Acts 19:11-12, ESV).* It was said of Jesus, no man can do such things except God be with him. And rightly so! It is the giver who chooses the vessels He will work through and the measure of anointing He will confer upon His servants. It is certainly not of ourselves lest we should take the praise.

7.9   "Here is Water, Baptise Me"

This end time move is to bring the world to salvation. The call to repentance is for all mankind. Whatever classification or status your birthing has given you matters not to God. He respects no man and the common man or those of high birth will all find themselves before God one day. The gracious act of mercy by Jesus has raised fallen man from the spiritual pits they are lodged in. When a thirsty soul is seeking the Water of Life, God will reveal Himself to them.

The eunuch, a man of eminence in the treasury of the household of Queen Candace (Acts 8:27) was on his way back to Ethiopia after being in Jerusalem to worship. He sat in the carriage reading about Jesus from the book of Isaiah. He did not have the understanding of the text and God who saw his enquiring heart responded accordingly. Phillip was told by an angel to go and meet with the eunuch on the road from Jerusalem to Gaza. It is God who connects people, and He destines those He is using to meet those who can help them. As he read the scriptures Phillip drew near and from that encounter the eunuch proclaimed "Here is water what hinders me from being baptised?" I believe there are many people around the world being led by the Spirit of God to read the Scriptures as they seek to know this same Jesus who introduced Himself to the eunuch those many centuries ago.

7.10 Walking, Leaping and Praising

On this account Peter and John entered the temple at the hour of prayer that is about 3pm in the afternoon. It was then they witnessed a crippled man being taken to the temple gates called

'Beautiful'. The cripple was being positioned in his usual place where daily he begged for money from those going into the temple courts.

As is customary he sought to beg Peter and John for money. Peter and John looked directly at him and Peter's quick response was to say 'Look at us!' His reaction got the full attention of the crippled man. *(6)"Peter said, "I have no silver and gold, but what I do have I give to you. In the name of Jesus Christ of Nazareth, rise up and walk!" (7)And he took him by the right hand and raised him up, and immediately his feet and ankles were made strong. (8)And leaping up he stood and began to walk, and entered the temple with them, walking and leaping and praising God." (Acts 3:6-8, ESV)*. It was for the glory of God and the people were amazed and spoke with wonder as they recognised the healed man to be the crippled courtyard beggar.

7.11   Crippled From Birth

In Acts 14:9-10) Paul and Barnabas on their travels through Iconium went into the synagogue to preach the Word. It was whilst boldly declaring the Good News that the unbelieving Jews incited the Gentiles onlookers to harm them. Iconium was a city divided against the apostles and the message of hope. The plot to harm them was already conceived in the hearts of those who were not for the apostles. The leaders were also privy to planning to hatch the plot against them. They conspired to mistreat and stone them. Paul and Barnabas when they heard what was being engineered against them quickly up and fled to Lystra and Derbe.

It was whilst in Lystra they came upon a crippled man who had no strength in his feet to stand. This man was lame from birth. As the impotent man listened to Paul preaching the Good News, Paul staring at him discerned that he had faith to be healed. Paul cried out "Stand up on your feet!" The crippled man immediately jumped up and began to walk.

7.12   Healing on Malta

Paul on his journey as a political prisoner was sailing in the Mediterranean when he and 274 seafarers met with a violent storm. They were eventually shipwrecked on the Island of Malta. The islanders were friendly and hospitable in welcoming him and the other passengers and mariners. The people became suspicious of him when a poisonous snake bit him, but he shook it off into the burning fire. This act made the islanders more curious about Paul because according to their folklore he should have keeled over and died. As that did not happen they deemed him to be an important man. As destiny would have it, the island's chief, Publius' father was suffering from dysentery and fever. It was in the mind of God that these people would witness His healing power and come to know that Jesus is Lord. In Acts 28:8, we see that Paul prayed for him, laid hands on him and he was healed.

7.13   Belonging to God

The apostles never ceased to follow in the footsteps of Jesus. They were empowered and anointed and great miracles were wrought as they went through the villages and cities of the nations.

Like the early crusaders of the faith we too can be extraordinary servants of the kingdom full of the Spirit if we follow the precepts of our faith. *"And I will give you a new heart, and a new spirit I will put within you. And I will remove the heart of stone from your flesh and give you a heart of flesh. And I will put my Spirit within you, and cause you to walk in my statutes and be careful to obey my rules" (Ezekiel 34: 26,27, ESV).*

We belong to God and the snare that held us captive has been broken. We have escaped as the bird from the snare of the evil fowler. Now we have this liberty in Christ Jesus, we walk not as those who do not know of this transforming power. *"And hope does not put us to shame, because God's love has been poured into our hearts through the Holy Spirit who has been given to us" (Romans 5:5, ESV).*

We are the last generation, and we will be emboldened by the Spirit to accomplish the end work of grace. We belong to God, and He desires that we come to repentance in this season of grace. *"Do you not know that you are God's temple and that God's Spirit dwells in you? If anyone destroys God's temple, God will destroy him. For God's temple is holy, and you are that temple" (1 Corinthians 3: 16-17, ESV)*. Like the apostles we are witnesses of what Christ has done for us. *"And we are witnesses to these things, and so is the Holy Spirit, whom God has given to those who obey him" (Acts 5:32, ESV)*. He has delivered, healed and given to us the ministry of reconciliation so that we can make disciples for the kingdom of God.

7.14   Bond of Iniquity

As servants of God, we will encounter many experiences with the kingdom of darkness. The people under the influence of evil, as was the case of Simon the sorcerer, are not privy to the spiritual battles because they are held captive in their sins. It is the work of those who are enlightened and delivered that is needed to help them to see the light.

In the *Collins English Dictionary,* the word *simony* means, the buying and selling of sacred or spiritual things. It is believed to have derived from the episode with Simon the sorcerer. He was artful in the skills of cunningness and trickery and seized upon the opportunity to buy the gift of God that Paul the apostle possessed. Paul's fierce retort was intended to rebuke the defiled spirit behind Simon's statement. It is an impudent action on the part of Simon that leads me to concur that such outrageous contempt towards the things of God can only be a provocation by the spirit of perversion.

This man, Simon Magnus although he claimed to be a christian is also thought to have established a church based on the teachings of Gnosticism. The earlier church had heretics within seeking to lead people astray from the Truth of Jesus' message. There were those who were under demonic control through witchcraft and the sin of iniquity. What is iniquity? According to *Strong's 4189, poneria* translates wickedness. It is certainly a sin that is generational and its consequences transferable with ensuing generations. Sin passes into the category of iniquity when there is rebellion and disobedience resulting from a long-term ignoring of the transgression. It is then passed from generation to generation. It is also a sin associated with witchcraft since rebellion is as the spirit of witchcraft (1 Samuel 15:23). Why is rebellion like witchcraft? The Bible says that when we do not believe the truth, we give entrance to the spirit of deception that is a lying spirit. Rebellion is a strongly rooted willful and defiant spirit.

Clearly, there is no transitional realm for us while we procrastinate over doing the right thing and repent. We do not act, think or speak outside of a spiritual realm. So if you believe the truth of God's Word, you belong to the kingdom of light. If you open yourself to not believing God's Word, you are under the influence of the kingdom of darkness. What God loved about His servant David the Psalmist was the position of his heart towards his sin. David postured before God in anguish and torment when he erred so miserably before God. The sin of iniquity is willful disobedience and neglect in amending one's ways. Simon mesmerised the people with his divination announcing himself as the 'great power of God' a false Messianic title.

7.15 Counterfeit Spirits

In the last days, many shall come claiming to be the Christ. It is an audacious spirit of deception to take the glory. We are warned to be vigilant in the spirit so that we are not deceived by these personalities. How do we know it is the voice of God? Firstly, the Bible says that there is safety in numbers. The counsel of God is important to remain alert and discerning in the spirit. We need to possess a spiritual mind to weigh with caution what is being presented, based solely on the Word of God. If what is being said does not align unequivocally with the Scriptures we must reject it. The end time will be a time of great challenges for Christians to remain true to the Word of God. We are encouraged that *"Where there is no guidance, a people falls, but in an abundance of counselors there is safety." (Proverbs 11:14, ESV).* In Luke 18:8, the question is asked whether the Son of Man will find faith when He comes. It is a pertinent point to consider because the pressure of the times will test the faith of those who are called the people of God and sadly, many will "burn out" under the spiritual provocation.

We are admonished to stand surefooted for God. As the mountain goat stands precariously on the steep incline of the rocky surface, it is able to remain steady because its feet are designed to grip the rocky surface. The mountain goat will survive on the open expanse prevailing against the harsh climate because of its tenacious grip. It is without a doubt that many will be challenged to stand on some steep slopes of faith. We can allude to the words of the song, "On Christ the solid rock we are able to stand." All other grounds will prove unstable as the cliff slopes crumble under testing and hope is lost. God will come through because His Word is sure.

PART EIGHT

A NEW SEASON

(15)"Until the Spirit is poured upon us from on high, and the wilderness becomes a fruitful field, and the fruitful field is deemed a forest. (16)Then justice will dwell in the wilderness, and righteousness abide in the fruitful field. (17) And the effect of righteousness will be peace, and the result of righteousness, quietness and trust forever.

(Isaiah 32:15-17, ESV)

8.1   The Covering of Peace

When life is parched, stagnant and there are no prospects of life, people seek out new habitations. It presents many challenges to move away from the familiar. However, the human spirit becomes dissatisfied and uncomfortable in environments that are not conducive to survival. The global calamities, tragedies, migratory problems and financial chaos are bringing people of all nations to their threshold of coping. I believe that just about everyone has a tale of displacement and human woe to tell. Our shared experiences are an indication of our similarities rather than differences.

God loves His creation, and we are secured in His protection when we come to know Him as Lord.

The peace of God prevails over all the global tremors of war and conflict. National atrocities, terror attacks, epidemics, earthquakes on scales not imaginable. There is widespread suffering and misery in the nations and these events are the works of evil. The author of the Psalm finds solace in the fact that his consolation is in the abiding covering of God's peace. Even though there will be shakings and convulsions that carry the earth into the sea, and mountains will be moved from their stock, we are assured to be still and know that Jesus is God. *"...(1) God is our refuge and strength, a very present help in trouble. (2) Therefore we will not fear though the earth gives way, though the mountains be moved into the heart of the sea, (3) though its waters roar and foam, though the mountains tremble at its swelling. Selah."* The word 'selah' here means to 'pause' (*Strong's Hebrew H5542*). After the dramatic and fearfully descriptive earth-moving verses, we are introduced to the calm and peace of these verses; *(4)"There is a river whose streams make glad the city of God, the holy habitation of the Most High. (5) God is in the midst of her; she shall not be moved; God will help her when morning dawns" (Psalms 46:1-5, ESV).*

We need not fear because the Lord is with us. The unshakeable confidence in our Lord must remain even when the complexities of untold human suffering is upon us. *"What have we to fear, what have we to dread leaning on the Everlasting Arm?"* Jesus the Prince of Peace is ever near to calm the raging seas that churn and spit fury at us. The dark waters of evil that have risen up to engulf our souls in these pressing times must recede at His rebuke. *"And he awoke and rebuked the wind and said to the sea, "Peace! Be still!" And the wind ceased, and there was a great calm. (Mark 4:39, ESV).*

Jesus is speaking to the angry seas in your life, *"Peace! Be still and know that I am God"* because He is the Captain of our faith. No demon can destroy this ship as it ploughs through the angry seas of time. It is on course to its final destination, the eternal harbour of rest in God.

8.2   A Great Movement

The season of God's glory has dawned upon mankind. We are in the time of His power and His glory. The current climate has been one of intimidation and fear as nations splinter at the joints and fragment under the ensuing pressures. The global landscape is one of a great upheaval of people, social challenges causing migratory movement and meltdown in seemingly impregnable national and financial pillars.

The order of the global arena will soon change as God shows His high arm of deliverance for His people. It has been a long night and soon will break the dawn.

The nations are coming to Jesus. The great movement of people and world chaos is a part of the great scheme of the end-time move of God. Although evil has orchestrated the movement through wars and instability, it coincides with the spiritual movement in the heavens as the great battle between good and evil rages into a climaxing season of the church age. The dispensation of salvation is swiftly drawing to a close. Everything is rapidly moving into the fullness and completeness of all things under the leadership of Jesus Christ, the Head of the Church as indicated in Ephesians 1.

106

8.3   The Healing Flow

Isaiah encapsulates in the verses below of Isaiah 32:15-18, the abundance of fruitfulness and the hope that comes through the refreshing of the eternal promise to us. The spirit within is energised and drawn like a magnet to the descriptive reference of hope and expectation of the Spirit's refreshing of salvation and healing. It is for this season. These prophetic utterances will now become a reality as men languish at the dry and thirsty dust bowls where the waters have become stagnant and putrid. *"They shall be healed and everything shall live, wherever the river cometh." (John 5:9 KJV).*

Life can be paralleled with the savannahs and the rainforests where the joy of summer gives way to the longing for the rainy season as the stench of death lingers in the air. The drought continues to claim the lives of the animals as they gather at the receding water holes desperate to quench their thirst. Water is a pivotal source for the sustaining of life. *"Jesus said unto her, I am the resurrection, and the life: he that believes in me, though ye were dead yet shall ye live" (John 11:25,KJV).* Jesus is the sustainer of our lives and when we were in our trespasses and sins He came and showered us with the water of life. For many who have come to salvation, we have the privilege to drink from the eternal source. It is a perpetual life flowing stream that cannot run dry. We can draw from the source in season or out of season.

"There is a river, the streams whereof shall make glad the city of God, the holy place of the tabernacles of the most High" (Psalms 46:4,American KJV). There is no languishing for thirst in the presence of our Lord. Those at the spiritual watering pools are as the living amongst the dead. When King David was faced with the prospects of being in the deserts of Judah, his narrative of the dusty, dry, and featureless landscape drew an image of his spiritual state. In that desolately barren and thirsty land, he thirsted for God. His experience perhaps caused him to see how wretched and joyless his spiritual self was before God, and he sought for a refreshing. We can rejoice with expectation in the prophetic words of Isaiah. *"Until the Spirit be poured upon us from on high, and the*

wilderness be a fruitful field and the fruitful field is deemed a forest. Then justice shall dwell in the wilderness, and righteousness abide in the fruitful field. And the effect of righteousness shall be peace: and the result of righteousness quietness and trust forever. My people will abide in a peaceable habitation, in sure dwelling, and in quiet resting places" (Isaiah 32: 15-18, ESV).

8.4 'The Well is Deep'

Jesus is referred to as the "water of life." If Jesus is the water of life that springs from the eternal wells then there can be no decay or death in Him. We will be eternally refreshed. When Jesus went to the well where He met the Samaritan woman, it was not by chance that they met. Like so many other bible characters, their paths were crossed by destiny. It was in the plan of God for His glory.

The discourse between Jesus and this woman is a revelation of the prejudices and stereotyping of groups in bible times. A Jewish man speaking with a woman, and a woman of Samaria! That was forbidden. She exclaimed, *"How is it that you, a Jew, ask for a drink from me, a woman of Samaria?"* The Jews did not associate with the Samaritans and in Scripture, they were often referred to in a derogatory manner. (Matthew 15:21-18). Jesus came to break down the social barriers and to bring people together through the common denominator of salvation, yet at times what he said seemed a contradiction. However, His statements may seem paradoxical but His meanings are saliently bearing out a point. An example is that of the Canaanite mother whose daughter was demon possessed. (Matthew 15:22-28). Initially it appears Jesus ignored her plea and his disciples were less than gracious towards her. The persistence of the woman even when it seemed she is being insulted did not deter her. Her great level of faith catches His attention. Faith cross all social boundaries and is the key to His mercy.

Now, back to the woman at the well. Jesus remarked to her, *"If you knew the gift of God, and who it is that is saying to you, 'Give me a drink,' you would have asked him, and he would have given you living water."* She is somewhat missing His point at times but Jesus goes beyond the talk, and He sees a woman with a pure heart. The religious leaders would condemn her just based on her lifestyle. She would not have stood a chance to engage in conversation with them. In her locality, she was probably known as a corrupt woman and the tongues would be constantly wagging. "Look at her she's talking to another man." "She is a disgrace." "How could He be seen speaking with such an immoral woman?" Jesus, however, was different and His presence was enthralling. He was like a magnet drawing those on the fringes of their society to Him. They loved Him as we do our Lord. *"The woman said to him, 'Sir, you have nothing to draw water with, and the well is deep. Where do you get that living water?'" (John 4:11, ASV). (13) "Jesus said to her, 'Everyone who drinks of this water will be thirsty again (14) but, whoever drinks of the water that I will give him will never be thirsty again. The water that I will give him will become in him a spring of water welling up to eternal life.'* The woman was excited and gushing forth with speech she said, to paraphrase, *"Give me that water you speak of so that I will not have to come back to these wells. I hate the daily chore of coming here to get water."* Jesus spoke of Himself as the Water of Life, and the flow is perpetually sourced from the presence of God. It is a well springing up within the spirit of man that gives eternal life.

The wells of our hearts are indeed deep. Our lives outside of the Giver are blocked stagnant wells. They are deep impassable subterraneans of evil. We do not know ourselves and we cannot move pass our pains and hurts without divine help. Only Jesus can go deep into the emotional, spiritual, and physical wells of our lives to the root cause of our spiritual and psychological obstructions. *"Counsel in the heart of man is like deep water; but a man of understanding will draw it out" (Proverbs 20:5, KJV).*

The scriptures in Psalms 95 verse 7, alludes to us being as a sheep in the hand of God. We can experience the protective care of our loving Father as He keeps us in the palm of His hands. Further, in the earlier verses mention is made of God's power in the earth. *"In His hand are the deep places of the earth; the heights of the mountains are his also" (Psalms 95:4, ASV).* Proverbially, our hearts can be descents of immeasurable corruption and equally insurmountable mountains of cares. Who can know the error of his ways except the Spirit reveals our true nature?

We are His creation and our phenomenal experiences over the course of life are inextricably linked to our Creator. Proverbs 21:1 reveals the power of God over our will and intents. This demolishes the argument for the existential self and puts into perspective the limitations of our human will to choose. We belong to God and He works in the affairs of our lives. *"The heart of the King is like a stream of waters in the hands of God, and he turns it wherever he chooses" (Aramaic Bible).* The heart is deep in His hands and the Spirit searches out the hidden things and makes them known so that we can deal with our denials and emotional baggage. The woman at the well went away rejoicing whilst inviting others to come and see a man I met at the well. He can transform your life with the power of God's love.

The work of grace in Jesus is to excavate from the ruins of our life experiences and to heal our entire being. The healing flow of the Spirit will shift the debris of life and free up the sub-terrains of our life wells. The Psalmist exclaimed, *"Oh taste and see that the Lord he is good and his mercies endure for ever."* The woman did not fully understand the narrative of Jesus, but I get a sense of her being drawn into the excitement that comes from being in His presence.

8.5   'Come, Drink Of Me'

The Great Feast of Tabernacles was a tradition of the yearly Jewish ceremonies instituted by God. *"Day after day, from the first day to the last, Ezra read from the Book of the Law of God. They celebrated the festival for seven days, and on the eighth day, in accordance with the regulation, there was an assembly" (Nehemiah 8:18, NIV).* It was at one of those feasts that Jesus used the platform to give the great invitation to those who longed for a spiritual quenching of their thirst. The yearly convocations and festivals were borne out of tradition and did not change the hearts of the people to long for a refreshing. Jesus' impromptu action caught the attention of the religious leaders who thought to bring him to the chief priests and Pharisees.

Jesus therefore, in His authority utilised the moment to deliver His invitation. *"On the last day of the feast, the great day, Jesus stood up..."(John 7)*. It was a common practice for the Priests to go by the water gate to the Pool of Siloam and fill a golden goblet with water. They would return as the music played and the people sang praises to God for bringing them out of captivity and the wilderness experience. The Priest would return and pour out the water into silver funnels as they sang Hosannas. It was markedly timed that Jesus got up during this feast of tradition and proclaimed with authority, *"... if anyone thirsts, let him come to me and drink" (John 7:37, ESV)*.

The pouring out of the water by the priests was significant of the promised Holy Spirit. Yet they rejected the Holy One who would make it all possible. The people needed the water of life. *"He who believes in me, as the Scripture has said, from within him will flow rivers of living water" (John 7:38, NIV)*. It is the role of the Spirit to replenish, revitalise, and rejuvenate the people from within. Prophetically, the living waters will cascade over the cliffs and rocks in us and the valleys and low plains of our experiences will be transformed into a spiritually fruitful landscape. The arid pools of our dead sea will teem once again with life as the times of refreshing come to mankind. The healing rains will flow and saturate the dusty byways of life. The floodgates of joy will open up. The wells of salvation will be unblocked for our healing and deliverance by the Spirit of God.

It will be a glorious time as the torrential flow of the ministry of reconciliation and healing tumbles and cascade down the mountain slopes of our Mount Herman into the desert plains of our lives. *"Then will the lame leap like a deer, and the mute tongue shout for joy. Water will gush forth in the wilderness and streams in the desert" (Isaiah 35:6, ESV)*. The healing flow of this end time experience will be momentous as the nations come to salvation. The seven seas represent the nations of the entire earth and water promotes life. To be in Jesus our Lord is exhilarating as we approach the rapture of the saints. Salvation and healing will be a great movement that will be unstoppable. It is God directed and no purposes of God can be restrained.

8.6   The Water is Stirred

For an angel went down at a certain time into the pool and stirred up the water; then whoever stepped in first, after the stirring of the water, was made well of whatever disease he had" (John 5:4, ESV). The waters of the nations have been stirred as the Spirit of God moves over the face of our human deeps. The momentous time has come for global salvation and healing as never seen in the earth. There can be no excuse for not stepping into the churning waters of healing. It is for all who will take the step of faith. Jesus is Lord of His harvest and He is calling men to repentance and wholeness.

References:

Strong's Greek/Hebrew Dictionary

'Leprosy' Wikipedia

Collins Dictionary

Merriam-Webster Dictionary

William Cowper, Wikipedia

Simon Magnus, Wikipedia

Matthew Henry Concise Commentary